ACKNOWLEDGEMENTS

We wish to thank the Metropolitan Police Service (MPS) and the Mayor's Office for Policing And Crime (MOPAC), who provided extensive access to their collections. In particular, we would like to thank the following for their support and advice: Martin Tunstall of MOPAC; all those at MPS who assisted, particularly Paul Bickley and Martin Hewitt; the London Policing Ethics Panel, particularly Professor Leif Wenar and Baroness Berridge; Alan Moss, Keith Skinner and Lindsay Siviter at the Crime Museum, who along with Paul Bickley helped with our access to the collections and unfailingly answered our many questions. Any errors are ours alone. We would also like to thank all the lenders: MOPAC and MPS, Robert Duncan, the Swanson family, Essex Police Museum, Wandsworth Prison Museum and particularly Stewart McLaughlin, who shared his extensive knowledge of the history and use of the execution box. At the Museum of London we would like to thank all our many colleagues and the project team, in particular Annette Day, Louise Doughty, Zey Kussan, Sean O'Sullivan, Jon Readman, Maria Rego, Frazer Swift and Finbarr Whooley. Special mention must go to Sean Waterman in the picture library and John Chase and Richard Stroud, who spent many hours at the Crime Museum photographing the collections. Our thanks to our editors and designers at I.B.Tauris: Anne Jackson, Lucy Morton, Robin Gable and Clare Martelli. Finally our thanks to our families, and in particular to Allan and Tim.

THE CRIME MUSEUM UNCOVERED

THE CRIME MUSEUM UNCOVERED

INSIDE SCOTLAND YARD'S
SPECIAL COLLECTION

JACKIE KEILY & JULIA HOFFBRAND

I.B.TAURIS
LONDON · NEW YORK

Published on occasion of the exhibition
The Crime Museum Uncovered, Museum of London
(9 October 2015–10 April 2016)

Published in 2015 by
I.B.Tauris & Co. Ltd
London · New York

www.ibtauris.com

ISBN   978 1 78130 041 1

A full CIP record for this book is available from the British Library
A full CIP record is available from the Library of Congress
Library of Congress Catalog: available

Designed and typeset in Avenir by illuminati, Grosmont
Printed and bound by Printer Trento, Italy

FSC
www.fsc.org

MIX
Paper from
responsible sources
FSC® C015829

CONTENTS

THEMES

CONCLUSION

PREFACE

This book, and the exhibition that inspired it, came about as a result of a collaboration between the Metropolitan Police Service, the Mayor's Office for Policing And Crime and the Museum of London. The Metropolitan Police wanted to explore ways of making the Crime Museum's collections – located at New Scotland Yard and not open to the public – accessible. The book is more than just a catalogue to accompany the exhibition; we have tried to create a work that stands independently and will continue to be relevant long after the doors to the exhibition have closed. Most importantly, this is the first time that many of the Crime Museum's objects have been seen in public and the first time that so many have been assembled together.

The Metropolitan Police's Crime Museum was founded in the mid-1870s. It was, and continues to be, used as a teaching collection for newly trained officers. It has never been open to the general public. The Museum's origins lie in the then recently established legal requirement for prisoners' property to be kept for them until their release, which led to the setting up of a special store for all property seized during an investigation. Eventually, from this came the Museum, as unclaimed items were put into a training collection which was then put on display for new recruits and guests to view.

Application can be made to the Metropolitan Police for access (and they are inundated with requests), but it is largely other police forces, those with a direct relationship to a case, or specially invited guests, who gain entry. The Museum visitors' books, which cover most of its 140-year history, bear witness to the variety of guests who have viewed the collection: from members of the royal family, Sir Arthur Conan Doyle, Gilbert & Sullivan and Houdini to the Australian cricket team of 1893. However, the vast majority of visitors

◄ **The Crime Museum** in 1883, from the *Illustrated London News*.

were, and continue to be, members of the Metropolitan Police Service and other police forces, or those involved in the process of the law.

The Museum's collection is not comprehensive. It developed in an ad hoc manner over the years, often depending on the individual interests of the curator or the availability of material. This means that it is not a complete history of policing in London, nor a comprehensive look at crime in the capital. The collection does, however, highlight the wide variety of crimes investigated by the Metropolitan Police in London, containing a broad span of cases which illustrate their long history and involvement in major investigations. One of the fascinating facts about the Metropolitan Police is that since 1842 they have had a special detective squad that can be called upon by other police forces throughout the United Kingdom; this has meant that many Metropolitan Police detectives have worked on cases that occurred outside London (two examples of this are the murder of Emily Kaye in 1924 near Eastbourne, and the Great Train Robbery of 1963, which occurred in Buckinghamshire). Nevertheless, given the force's London location, most of the featured cases are London-based. So, although not comprehensive, this is a remarkable and very special collection of the history of crime investigation in the United Kingdom.

As museum curators, we were extremely excited to be given the opportunity to create an exhibition from this collection. The challenges were many: what criminal cases to include; what items to select; how should these be arranged; and, above all, how to ensure that the victims' voices were heard. These were extremely difficult decisions and not undertaken easily. We knew that there was a limited public knowledge of the Crime Museum, both from existing books (such as Gordon Honeycomb's two volumes on the collections, and one by Bill Waddell, a previous curator of the Museum), and from often unreliable sources on the internet. This meant that there would be an expectation of seeing certain objects which had been publicised as being in the Museum. It also meant that there were certain fallacies about the Museum and its collections that we could use the exhibition to correct.

We were given free rein by the Metropolitan Police to select whatever objects we wanted to use. The complete number of items held in the Crime Museum is estimated to be in the region of 2,000.

From this we selected just under 600 to include in the exhibition. About 400 of these are included in this book. In the beginning we considered every object and gradually decided on how we would select the criminal cases and present the accompanying objects. We knew it would be important to include the famous cases – such as Jack the Ripper, Dr Crippen, John Christie, the Krays and the Great Train Robbery – but we were keen also to display cases that led to major developments in detection methods and forensics, or that had helped to change the law. We were lucky that, because this is a teaching collection, it included many such cases. Finally we also felt it was important to include stories that reflected more ordinary crime in London, those crimes and victims that are often forgotten. Above all, we wanted the victims, and those who had investigated and solved these cases, to feature prominently. But we did not want to cause undue distress to any victims. We decided that in selecting cases to look at in detail we would not select any that postdated 1975, one hundred years after the founding of the Crime Museum. With broader themes, although we do not focus on particular individuals we decided to include cases that were relatively recent, hence the inclusion of the 7 July London bombings and the 2007 London and Glasgow Airport incidents.

The Crime Museum's collections include items that date back to the original Crime Museum of the late nineteenth century. We felt, therefore, that one of the first sections of the exhibition should contain these early collections. Few images exist of the earliest incarnations of the Museum, so we created a gallery for the exhibition that reflected the spirit of the early Museum, containing some features that are recognisable from the surviving pictures. All of the material predating 1905 was selected for inclusion in this section. This includes perhaps the most notorious of London crime cases, that of Jack the Ripper. There have long been rumours that the Crime Museum contained missing letters or items associated with the investigation. We hope here to have ended that speculation by showing all of the Crime Museum's Jack the Ripper collection: an appeal-for-information poster, a police notice to householders, and a number of items associated with known possible suspects who were convicted of other crimes (such as Frederick Deeming, Dr Neil Cream, George Chapman, and Michael Ostrog). This material appears in the first section, which also includes a small number of objects that predate the setting up of the Metropolitan Police Service in 1829 as well as objects added to the collections that do not directly relate to the Metropolitan Police – for example, the snuff box allegedly owned by the murderer John Thurtell, dating to the early 1820s; or the death masks from Newgate Prison, a number of which relate to City of London Police investigations (the City of London maintains its own police service, which is independent of the Metropolitan Police).

The main part of the collection originated after 1900. Here we decided to select a number of individual criminal cases that would shed light on particular developments in policing or changes in the law. All of these cases were well known in their time and many are still notorious today. We ended up with twenty-four of these, spanning most of the twentieth century: from the Stratton Brothers case of 1905 to the Spaghetti House siege of 1975. We also wanted to present material that reflected both the changing role of the Metropolitan Police and the nature of the crimes they have to deal with. We decided therefore to select material illustrating a number of themes: offensive and disguised weapons, drugs, firearms, abortion, capital punishment, terrorism, public protest, espionage, burglary and robbery, counterfeiting and forgery, as well as aspects of police procedures. Some themes, such as abortion, reflect a crime that has completely altered due to changes in the law. The selection of themes once again reflects the objects within the Museum's collections – some possible themes, such as prostitution or illegal gambling, were either not represented or had not been sufficiently collected.

In selecting both the items and the criminal cases, the Museum of London thought carefully about what was appropriate to include. We consulted our partners, the Metropolitan Police Service and the Mayor's Office for Policing And Crime, and we also took advice from the London Policing Ethics Panel, which gives independent advice on ethical matters relating to policing in London. Above all else, we did not want to bring further distress to victims of crime. Therefore, in addition to not looking in detail at any individual cases after 1975, we also decided against including any human remains (as specified by

▶ **New Scotland Yard** building of 1890.

the Human Tissue Act). In addition, through the police and where appropriate, we contacted the families of the victims who are featured.

We hope that we have done justice to this remarkable collection and to the people whom it represents. The individual items bear witness to many lives, and reveal many stories. Often these are the stories of the famous and the infamous, but they are also stories about Londoners that are often untold – about offenders, victims and police officers. Crimes against women feature prominently. These stories are often uncomfortable, even disturbing, but they provide an important insight into the diverse aspects of London's history.

Jackie Keily & Julia Hoffbrand

EARLY YEARS OF THE METROPOLITAN POLICE

1829 METROPOLITAN POLICE ACT

An Act for improving the Police in and near the metropolis

Created a centralised police force which soon numbered 3,000 men under the authority of the Home Secretary, Robert Peel. Responsible for policing the entire metropolitan area except the City of London. Previous policing in London relied on private individuals, salaried officials and semi-official 'thief-takers'. Headquarters at 4 Whitehall Place, Westminster. It soon became known as 'Scotland Yard' because its main public entrance was at its rear in Great Scotland Yard.

▶ 5 Divisions

▶ 8 Superintendents

▶ 20 Inspectors

▶ 88 Sergeants

▶ 895 Constables

Metropolitan Police officers soon became known as 'bobbies' or 'Peelers' after Robert Peel.

1842 DETECTIVE BRANCH

Followed public outcry over escape by murderer Daniel Good and an assassination attempt on Queen Victoria.

8 Detectives:

▶ Inspector Nicholas Pearce

▶ Inspector John Hayes

▶ Sergeant William Gerrett

▶ Sergeant Frederick Shaw

▶ Sergeant Charles Burgess Goff

▶ Sergeant Stephen Thornton

▶ Sergeant Jonathan Whicher

▶ Sergeant John Braddick

▲ **Robert Peel**
by Sir Thomas Lawrence.

c.**1870**   PRISONERS' PROPERTY STORE

Established at Scotland Yard to safeguard convicted prisoners' property.

c.**1875**   THE POLICE MUSEUM

Inspector Percy Neame has long been credited with creating the Police Museum from items deposited at the Prisoners' Property Store.

1878   CRIMINAL INVESTIGATION DEPARTMENT (CID)

Formed after the notorious 1877 corruption scandal 'Trial of the Detectives'. It replaced the Detective Branch.
Divisional Detective sections:
▶ 15 Detective Inspectors
▶ 159 Detective Sergeants
Central Detective Branch at Scotland Yard:
▶ 1 Detective Superintendent
▶ 3 Chief Inspectors
▶ 20 Detective Inspectors
▶ 6 Detective Sergeants and Detective Constables

1890   NEW SCOTLAND YARD BUILDING, VICTORIA EMBANKMENT

New Metropolitan Police headquarters. Purpose-built because the police had outgrown Whitehall Place and Great Scotland Yard buildings. The Police Museum moved to New Scotland Yard.

1901   FINGERPRINT BUREAU

Created by Assistant Commissioner Edward Henry. Headed by Detective Inspector Charles Stedman supported by Detective Sergeant Charles Stockley Collins and Detective Constable Frederick Hunt.

1902   DETECTIVES' TRAINING SCHOOL

Small training school for detectives opened at the New Scotland Yard building.

▲ **An early Peeler.**

▲ **Limehouse CID** investigating drug smuggling in disguise, c. 1911.

HISTORY OF THE CRIME MUSEUM

The Crime Museum's origins go back to legal changes in the late 1860s and early 1870s which required that prisoners' property be kept for them until they were released from prison and free to claim it. By 1874 items seized by the Metropolitan Police during an investigation and still held by them after conviction were sent to a Prisoners' Property Store at Scotland Yard.

Most property was never claimed and the store was soon stocked from cellar to roof with items relating to crimes. It is believed that in about 1875 Inspector Percy Neame, who was employed at the store, began setting aside objects to form a training collection for new officers. From its creation, this 'Police Museum' was open only to those involved in the administration of the criminal law, or by special invitation.

By 1876 journalists were fuelling their readers' imaginations with dark descriptions of the museum's contents, such as weapons, burglary tools, false beards and forged banknotes. Many reporters commented on the museum's cleanliness and order, with each item labelled and dusted with disinfectant powder. Some sighed with relief as they escaped into the outside air. By 1877 the press were calling it the 'Black Museum' to reflect its sinister contents.

Over the Museum's 140-year life its name and its location within Scotland Yard have changed. However, it remains a place of mystery and fascination for the public. To the Metropolitan Police community it is a source of instruction, remembrance and respect.

THE EARLY CRIME MUSEUM

THE EARLY CRIME MUSEUM

In 1894 the museum was open by order of the Commissioner, Sir Edward Bradford, for two hours in the afternoons of Mondays, Tuesdays, Thursdays and Fridays. It was located in the New Scotland Yard building designed by Norman Shaw on the Embankment.

Except for when the museum was closed during the two world wars, its visitors' book has been kept continuously since 1877. The volumes paint a vivid picture of the museum's many guests over its 140-year history. Sandwiched between lesser-known individuals are a colourful mix of police officers, writers, celebrities, politicians, kings and queens, many from far across the globe.

The volume opposite is open at page 1 and shows the signature of Sir Edmund Henderson, the second Commissioner of the Metropolitan Police. Beneath this are the signatures of his Assistant Commissioner, Lieutenant-Colonel Douglas Labalmondière, and Captain William C. Harris.

◄ **Crime Museum sign**
8 May 1894.

▼ **Crime Museum visitors' book**
Volume 1, 1877–1904.

▼ **Crime Museum catalogue**
late nineteenth century.

On 26 July 1892 Tom Bullen appears with his boss, John Moore. Bullen is the journalist many at the time believed wrote the 'Dear Boss' letter which gave the Whitechapel murderer the name Jack the Ripper.

The museum's catalogue contains a wealth of information about its early collections. Press cuttings about the museum and relevant cases are pasted inside next to neat handwritten object entries. The first items listed, for example, are 'Jemmies: Housebreaking implements found in the possession of two burglars on "P or Walworth Division" sentenced at Central Criminal Court 5th February 1864'.

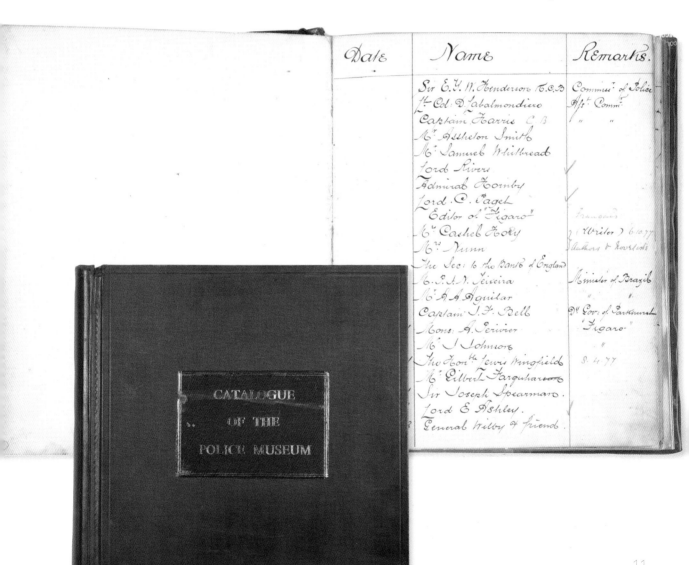

DEATH MASKS

These death masks, made from plaster of Paris, were created after executions at Newgate Prison and formed part of a collection there. When Newgate closed in 1902 they were acquired by the Crime Museum. Some were produced for phrenological purposes, to study the shape of a convict's head. Others were made as curios to record the faces of notorious criminals, not unlike the making of the wax figures at Madame Tussaud's.

In 1824, the murderer John Thurtell (see p. 39) requested that when his body went for dissection for medical purposes after he was executed, a cast of his face should not be taken in case it ended up as a bust and was later seen by his family. Consequently the Phrenologial Society in London was only allowed to make a cast of the back of his head.

Many of these masks were made by Bartholomew Casci, of 3 Harford Place, Drury Lane. In the 1851 Census he is described as a moulder and figure maker. The death mask of James Greenacre was made two days after his death in May 1837 by J. Miller of Theobald's Road in Holborn. This area was known for its modellers and makers of plaster casts.

THOMAS WICKS 1846

Thomas Wicks, 20, was an apprentice to James Bostock, 46, a brass founder of Drury Lane. Wicks lost money that a customer had given him for Bostock, for which he was rebuked. Two days later Wicks arrived for work at Bostock's home and shot him in the head. Wicks then wandered off around the neighbourhood before being arrested in a coffee shop. He was found guilty and hanged outside Newgate Prison on 30 March 1846.

JAMES GREENACRE 1837

In late December 1836, a female torso was found in a bag on the Edgware Road. In early January, a woman's head was recovered from the Regent's Canal. The head and body were found to be from the same woman. A month later the victim's legs were found in Camberwell. In March, Hannah Brown's brother identified the remains as his missing sister.

James Greenacre, 42, later to become known as the 'Edgware Road Murderer', had been engaged to Hannah Brown, 47. But his main interest was in her money, as he also had a mistress, Sarah Gale. He and Gale were arrested: he was tried for murder, and she as an accessory after the fact. Both were found guilty: Greenacre was hanged on 2 May 1837 outside Newgate Prison and Gale was transported to Australia for life. This death mask was made on 4 May by J. Miller of Theobald's Road.

DANIEL GOOD 1842

On 7 April 1842, a pair of trousers was stolen in Wandsworth. PC Gardner went to a nearby large house where the coachman, Daniel Good, 46, was suspected of the crime. In the stables, PC Gardner found the headless and limbless torso of a woman: Good's common-law wife Jane Jones, 40. Good locked the officer in the stable and escaped, but was arrested about ten days later in Kent.

The police were heavily criticised in the press for the delay in catching Good. He was tried and hanged at Newgate Prison on 23 May 1842. The case led directly to the formation of a dedicated detective team within the Metropolitan Police.

ROBERT BLAKESLEY 1841

James Burdon, 38, was the landlord of the King's Head public house on Eastcheap when he was attacked by Robert Blakesley, 27. Burdon's wife was the sister of Blakesley's wife, who had moved back into the King's Head to escape her husband. Blakesley attacked his wife, injuring her, and then stabbed to death his brother-in-law, who had been sleeping but awoke on hearing the commotion.

Blakesley came from a well-to-do family; his father was a cloth merchant in the City of London. However, he had a history of mental illness and by the time of the murder was in financial trouble. He was hanged outside Newgate Prison on 15 November 1841.

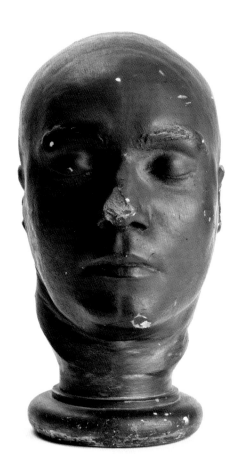

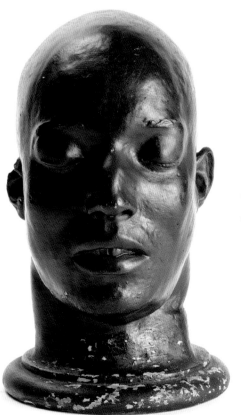

THOMAS HOCKER 1845

The body of James De La Rue, 27, was found in fields in Hampstead on the evening of 21 February 1845. He had been beaten to death. Shortly afterwards a man, Thomas Hocker, 22, approached the police officer who was guarding the body, offering him brandy and money, but did not admit to knowing the dead man.

It later transpired that they had been best friends who had fallen out over a woman, known only as Caroline. Hocker wrote De La Rue a letter pretending to be the woman concerned, luring De La Rue to his place of death. The bloodstained letter was found in De La Rue's pocket. Hocker was hanged outside Newgate Prison on 28 April 1845. He fainted on his way to the scaffold and had to be supported during his execution.

THOMAS SALE 1848

On 11 October 1847, John Bellchambers was attacked and robbed by a gang near his home in Westminster. He later died from his wounds. Two of the gang, Thomas Sale and George McCoy, both aged 25, were found guilty of his murder. Sale was hanged outside Newgate Prison on 10 January 1848.

WILLIAM HEWSON 1848

William Hewson, 45, was a prisoner in Coldbath Fields Prison. He murdered William Woodhouse, one of the warders, on 10 June 1848, stabbing him in the heart. Hewson was serving a two-year sentence for concealing the birth of a child, the result of an incestuous relationship with his daughter. The child had died and he had disposed of the body. Hewson was hanged outside Newgate Prison on 24 July 1848.

LUIGI BURANELLI 1855

Luigi Buranelli, 32, was lodging at a house in Foley Place, Marylebone. He was having an affair with another lodger, Mrs Williamson. There was an argument and he was asked to leave but returned some days later and shot his landlord, Joseph Lambert, whilst he slept in his bed.

Buranelli attempted suicide and was almost certainly suffering from some form of mental illness. He was hanged outside Newgate Prison on 30 April 1855. His mental health caused unease among many observers and a pamphlet, *The Case of Luigi Buranelli: Medico-legally Considered*, was published shortly after his death deploring his execution.

ROBERT MARLEY 1856

Richard Cope was working in a jeweller's in Parliament Street when Robert Marley, 39, tried to rob it. In trying to stop him, Cope was severely beaten and eventually died from his wounds. Marley was caught by a member of the public as he tried to escape. He was found guilty and hanged at Newgate Prison on 15 December 1856. *The Times* reported that following his death a cast was made of his face and his clothes were burnt to stop them being put on public exhibition.

JAMES MULLINS 1860

Mary Elmsley, 70, was a wealthy widow. She was found murdered in her home off the Mile End Road. James Mullins, 52, had worked as an odd-job man for her and had previously served with the Metropolitan Police, although he had been let go due to a misdemeanour. Mullins came forward and tried to incriminate someone else but ended up being arrested himself. He was found guilty and was hanged outside Newgate Prison on 19 November 1860 before a crowd of around 20,000 people.

FRANZ MULLER 1864

Franz Muller, 24, was a German tailor living in London. In July 1864 he attacked Thomas Briggs, 69, in the first-class compartment of a North London railway train travelling from Fenchurch Street to Chalk Farm. He robbed him, beat him and threw him from the train. Briggs died a short time later. His was the first British railway murder.

Muller was tracked down through a gold chain he had stolen from Briggs, but by this time he was already on his way to America. Detective Inspector Richard Tanner travelled on a faster ship to New York with two witnesses, who identified Muller when he finally landed there. An interesting feature of the case was that Muller had left his own hat at the crime scene and had taken Briggs's tall top hat. When he arrived in America he had the hat with him but had cut the crown down to form a shallower hat. This became known as a 'Muller Cut Down' and become a fashionable style. Muller was brought back to Britain, found guilty and hanged outside Newgate Prison on 14 November 1864. The case highlighted fears about railway travel and led to the introduction a few years later of the communication cord to stop the train in case of emergency.

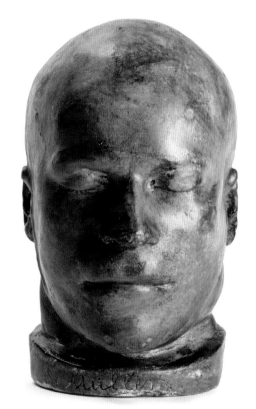

EXECUTIONS

In 1783 public hangings in London moved from a tree at Tyburn to a scaffold outside Newgate Prison. Large crowds would gather to watch the executions, and those who could afford to do so rented rooms overlooking the scene. In 1868 public hangings ended and executions were moved to within the prison walls.

When Newgate closed in 1902 its gallows were transferred to Pentonville Prison for men and Holloway Prison for women. From 1878 those who were sentenced to death south of the River Thames were hanged at Wandsworth Prison.

ROPE USED TO HANG JOHN PLATTS
for the murder of George Collis, 1847

John Platts, 22, was hanged at Derby by Samuel Haywood on 1 April 1847 for the murder of George Collis. Haywood had been offered the job of hangman for Leicestershire, Derbyshire and Nottinghamshire while he was imprisoned in Leicester prison in 1817 for poaching. He travelled all over the country to conduct hangings.

ROPE USED TO HANG WILLIAM SEAMAN
for the murder of Jonathan Levy, 1896

On 4 April 1896 Seaman, 46, attempted to rob the home of Jonathan Levy in Turner Street, Whitechapel. After battering to death Mr Levy and his housekeeper, Sarah Gale, Seaman tried to escape over neighbouring rooftops but was captured by police. Seaman's knife, chisel and hammer, which he used in the murders, appear in the museum's catalogue.

ROPE USED TO HANG MARY PEARCEY
for the murder of Phoebe Hogg, 1890

Mary Pearcey, 24, was hanged at Newgate Prison on 23 December 1890 for murdering her lover Frank Hogg's wife, Phoebe. She had also killed his 18-month-old daughter.

Mrs Hogg's body was discovered on 24 October 1890 in Crossfield Road, Hampstead. Her baby's body was found a mile away and a bloodstained pram nearby. Bloodstained knives and clothing were found in Mary Pearcey's kitchen in Camden Town. The case caused great public excitement and 30,000 people visited Mary Pearcey's waxwork in Madame Tussaud's when it was displayed soon after her execution.

This rope was given to the Crime Museum in 1892 by the governor of Holloway Prison.

19

Albert Milsom, 1896

Henry Fowler, 1896

ROPES USED TO HANG ALBERT MILSOM AND HENRY FOWLER

for the murder of Henry Smith, 1896

Albert Milsom, 33, and Henry Fowler, 31, were hanged together at Newgate Prison on 9 June 1896 for the murder of Henry Smith in Muswell Hill. William Seaman was hanged between them on the scaffold. He had been placed there to prevent Milsom and Fowler attacking each other.

'The Muswell Hill Murder' hit the headlines in February 1896 when Mr Smith's badly beaten body was found in his kitchen. He had been tied up and his safe ransacked. A bullseye lantern was found in the kitchen sink.

Descriptions of two men seen nearby shortly before the murder fitted those of Milsom and Fowler, who were known criminals. When Milsom's family was questioned his 15-year-old brother-in-law identified the lantern as his. Milsom and Fowler left London after the murder but were tracked down and arrested in a hostel in Bath. They were both armed with revolvers.

These ropes, and the ropes with which William Seaman and Amelia Dyer were hanged, were donated to the Crime Museum by Lieutenant Colonel Everard Millman, governor of Holloway Prison, in 1897.

This lantern was found in the kitchen sink near Mr Smith's body. Henry Miller, Milsom's brother-in-law, told police he had bought the lantern in Golborne Road, Notting Hill, and that he used to play with it in the evenings with his friends. On the night of the murder it went missing and he didn't see it again until the police questioned him about it. He added that the next day Milsom had instructed him to tell anyone asking that he had broken the lantern dusting it. The Crime Museum's catalogue describes the lantern as 'the article which gave the first clue to the murderers'.

Henry Miller testified at the trial that when he bought his lantern it had no wick, so he made one out of fabric his sister had used to make some children's dresses. He had put a penholder round the wick to stop it flaring too much. When Chief Inspector Henry Marshall compared the lantern's wick with the fabric of one of the dresses, they matched exactly, so verifying Henry's story.

▲ **Bullseye lantern** found in Henry Smith's kitchen, 1896.

◄ Wick and **cloth pieces** from the bullseye lantern, 1896.

ROPE USED TO HANG AMELIA DYER
for the murder of Doris Marmon, 1896

Amelia Dyer, 57, was hanged at Newgate on 10 June 1896 for the murder of 2-month-old Doris Marmon. She was one of the nineteenth century's most notorious 'baby farmers', individuals who in return for payment agreed to care for unwanted babies. These children were often born to poor or unmarried mothers.

On 31 March 1896 Dyer took charge of Doris from her mother, Evalina Marmon, in Cheltenham. Mrs Marmon gave Dyer £10 and a box of Doris's clothes. Instead of returning to the 'good and comfortable home' she had described to Mrs Marmon, Dyer went to 76 Mayo Road, Willesden, where her daughter Mary Ann lived with her husband Arthur Palmer. There, Dyer strangled Doris with white edging tape used in dressmaking. The next day she strangled 13-month-old Harry Simmonds, who had also been brought to Mayo Road for adoption. She carried the bodies by train to Reading in a carpet bag, weighted it down with bricks, and threw it into the River Thames.

Meanwhile a few days earlier, a package containing the body of a baby girl, Helena Fry, had been retrieved from the Thames at Reading. Detectives had deciphered a faintly legible name and address on the package. When Dyer was arrested on 4 April police found in her home white edging tape, pawn tickets for children's clothing, receipts for advertisements and letters from mothers asking about their children.

The Thames was dragged and six more babies' bodies were discovered, including those of Doris Marmon and Harry Simmons. It is unknown how many more children Dyer murdered.

EXECUTIONER WILLIAM MARWOOD

Marwood served as hangman to the Sheriffs of London and Middlesex from 1874 to 1883. He was originally a cobbler and began his career as a hangman, aged 54, at Lincoln Castle Prison in 1872. He is famous for developing the 'long drop' technique of hanging, which was considered more humane than the 'short drop'. He was one of only two executioners to give their name to the character of the hangman in the Punch and Judy puppet show (Jack Ketch being the other).

Marwood executed a number of notorious prisoners, including Henry Wainwright, who was hanged at Newgate Prison in 1875 for murdering his mistress Harriet Lane; Charles Peace, burglar and murderer, whom he hanged at Armley Prison in 1879; and Kate Webster, who was hanged at Wandsworth Prison, also in 1879, for murdering her employer.

Marwood's name appears in the Crime Museum's visitors book on 18 June 1883. In the address column he wrote simply 'hangman'.

In reply to a request for one of his ropes for the museum, Marwood writes that he never lets his ropes out of his hands or lets them be cut. He adds that the recipient of his letter can see a rope by coming to the prison.

WM. MARWOOD,

EXECUTIONER,

CHURCH LANE,

HORNCASTLE,

LINCOLNSHIRE, ENGLAND.

▲ William Marwood's business card, c.1876. His occupation is given as 'Executioner'. He continued to live at Church Lane, Horncastle, Lincolnshire, until his death.

▶ Letter from executioner William Marwood to the Police Museum, 20 August 1876.

23

THE JACK THE RIPPER MURDERS

Between April 1888 and February 1891, eleven women were brutally murdered in the East End of London by an unknown murderer or murderers. These murders caused widespread fear and panic in London and sparked Britain's largest ever murder investigation. Newspapers competed to report the most sensational stories and sell the most copies. The Whitechapel murderer became known as Jack the Ripper. He or she has never been identified.

On 7 October plain-clothes police officers made house-to-house searches in Whitechapel and Spitalfields. They left a copy of this notice at every house and tenement they visited. On 9 November another brutal murder was discovered. When the police finally closed their file on the Whitechapel Murders in 1891, four more women had been brutally killed.

The poster reproduces a letter dated 25 September 1888 written in blood-red ink which the Central News Agency said it received on 27 September. The poster asks anyone recognising the handwriting to contact the police. This so-called 'Dear Boss' letter gave the unknown murderer the name 'Jack the Ripper'. When the poster was published six women had already been viciously murdered.

The poster also reproduces a postcard written in red ink, dated 1 October, which was sent to the Central News Agency.

POLICE NOTICE.

TO THE OCCUPIER.

On the mornings of Friday, 31st August, Saturday 8th, and Sunday, 30th September, 1888, Women were murdered in or near Whitechapel, supposed by some one residing in the immediate neighbourhood. Should you know of any person to whom suspicion is attached, you are earnestly requested to communicate at once with the nearest Police Station.

Metropolitan Police Office,
30th September, 1888.

Printed by M'Corquodale & Co. Limited, "The Armoury," Southwark.

▲ **Metropolitan Police notice**, 30 September 1888.

▶ **Metropolitan Police appeal poster**, 3 October 1888.

METROPOLITAN POLICE.

Fac-simile of Letter and Post Card received by Central News Agency.

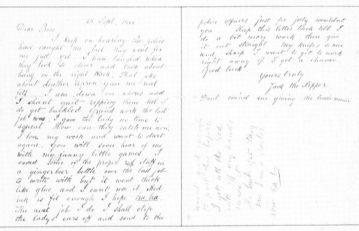

Any person recognising the handwriting is requested to communicate with the nearest Police Station.

Metropolitan Police Office,
3rd October, 1888.

Printed by M'Corquodale & Co. Limited, "The Armoury," Southwark.

DEATH MASK OF MURDERER FREDERICK DEEMING
1892

Deeming, a 38-year-old Englishman, was executed in Melbourne, Australia, on 23 May 1892 for the murder of his second wife Emily. It was discovered soon afterwards that he had previously murdered his first wife and four children in England and buried their bodies under floorboards. His long criminal career of thieving and obtaining money under false pretences led him to become a police suspect in the Jack the Ripper murders. It is said that the Australian authorities sent Scotland Yard this death mask in connection with this.

MEDICINE CASE
belonging to poisoner Dr Cream, c.1892

This drugs case belonged to Dr Thomas Neill Cream, a Scottish-born Canadian doctor, who was hanged at Newgate Prison on 15 November 1892 for poisoning Matilda Clover with strychnine. He had also used strychnine hidden in homeopathic pills to murder Ellen Donworth, 19; Alice Marsh, 21; and Emma Shrivell, 18.

At his trial another woman, Louise Harvey, testified that he had given her pills, which she had pretended to swallow but instead threw into the River Thames. Cream became known as the Lambeth Poisoner and within a week of his conviction his waxwork was on display at Madame Tussaud's wearing his own clothes.

It has been claimed that Cream's last words on the scaffold were 'I am Jack the…' This has led some to suspect him of being Jack the Ripper. However, he was in prison in America at the time of the murders.

POLICE CIRCULAR, March 1905
containing photograph of John Evest, suspected under
the alias Michael Ostrog in the Jack the Ripper case

This circular was issued by the Registrar of Habitual Criminals based
at the Convict Supervision Office, New Scotland Yard. Its purpose
was to alert officers to repeat offenders after their release.

Photograph no. 20 shows John Evest. Inside the circular his
aliases are listed as Matters Ostrog, Bertrand Ashley, Claude Cayton,
Staniston Sublinsky and Michael Ostrog. Five previous convictions
for stealing are noted, the most serious of which attracted a sentence
of ten years' imprisonment and seven years' supervision. He is
described as 5 foot 8¾ inches tall with dark brown hair, turning grey,
thin and brown eyes. Further remarks include 'Clever old thief. Gains
access to hospitals and medical colleges by introducing himself as a
friend of the father of one of the doctors or students, and when left
alone, steals valuable instruments. Also frequents military barracks
and steals from officers' quarters. Speaks with foreign accent, wears
pince-nez and walks feebly.'

In 1894 he was a suspect under the name Michael Ostrog in the
Jack the Ripper case and was detained as 'a homicidal maniac'.

CONVICT SUPERVISION OFFICE,

New Scotland Yard,

March, 1905.

ILLUSTRATED CIRCULAR, No. 76.

(TRAVELLING CRIMINALS.)

Issued by the Registrar of Habitual Criminals.

INDEX.

Printed by the Receiver for the Metropolitan Police District, New Scotland Yard, S.W.   890 4 | 1905.

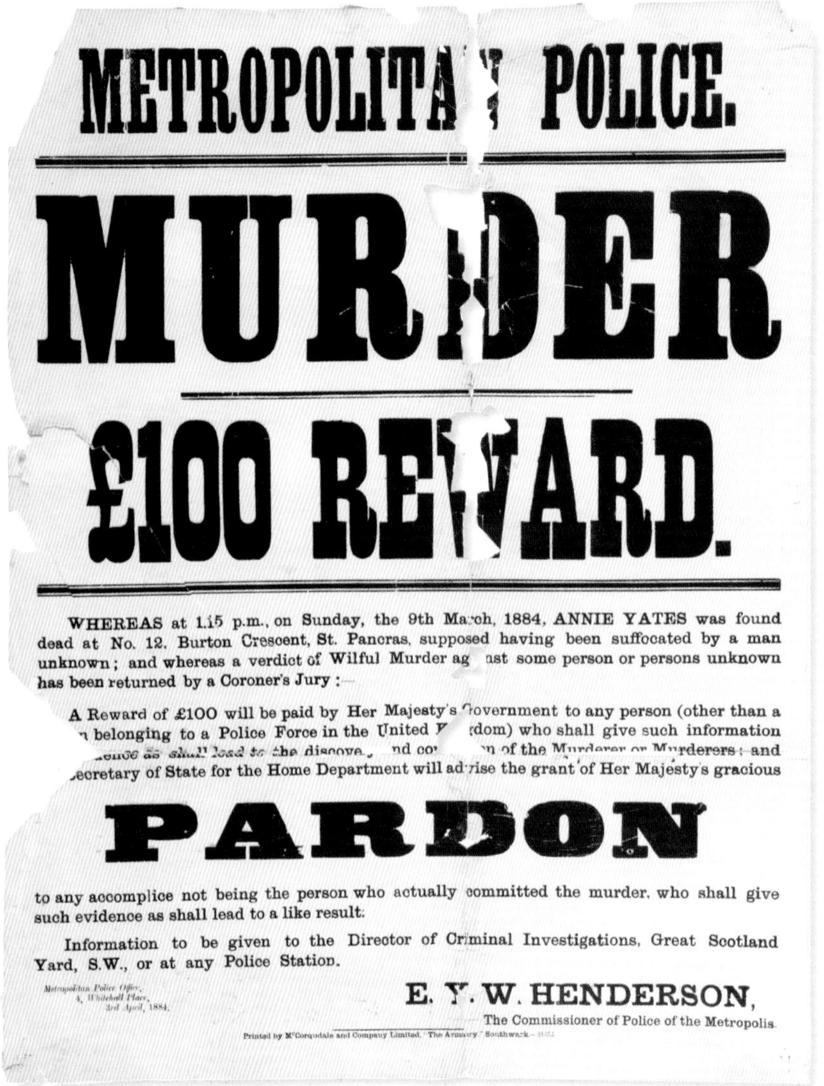

METROPOLITAN POLICE.

MURDER

£100 REWARD.

WHEREAS at 1.15 p.m., on Sunday, the 9th March, 1884, ANNIE YATES was found dead at No. 12, Burton Crescent, St. Pancras, supposed having been suffocated by a man unknown; and whereas a verdict of Wilful Murder against some person or persons unknown has been returned by a Coroner's Jury :—

A Reward of £100 will be paid by Her Majesty's Government to any person (other than a ~~n belonging to a Police Force in the United Kingdom~~) who shall give such information ~~...ence as shall lead to the discove...~~ nd co...n of the Murderer or Murderers; and ...ecretary of State for the Home Department will advise the grant of Her Majesty's gracious

PARDON

to any accomplice not being the person who actually committed the murder, who shall give such evidence as shall lead to a like result:

Information to be given to the Director of Criminal Investigations, Great Scotland Yard, S.W., or at any Police Station.

Metropolitan Police Office,
4, Whitehall Place,
3rd April, 1884.

E. Y. W. HENDERSON,
The Commissioner of Police of the Metropolis.

Printed by M'Corqudale and Company Limited, 'The Armoury,' Southwark.—2051

POSTER

appealing for information about the
murder of Annie Yates in 1884

The body of Mary Anne Yates was found at 12 Burton Crescent, St Pancras, on 9 March 1884. She had been hit on the head and strangled. It was thought she was killed by a man she had brought back to her room, but her murderer was never found.

This poster was produced by McCorqudale & Co., Southwark, who also printed the police appeal poster about Jack the Ripper. They were well-known printers of railway timetables and posters.

▲ **Textiles and hair** from the remains of a woman's body found in a barrel, 1880.

THE HARLEY STREET MYSTERY

On 3 June 1880 a female body was discovered in a barrel in the cellar of 139 Harley Street. The house was lived in by a merchant, Mr Jacob Henriques. The inquest established that the body had been there for more than a year and had probably been buried with a quantity of chloride of lime before being placed in the barrel. Fragments of textile and hair were recovered and casts were made of the jaw and teeth, but the identity of the woman was never discovered.

The victim was estimated to have been less than 5 ft tall and was aged between 30 and 40. She appeared to have died from a stab wound. It was thought that she may have been a prostitute who was brought back by one of the servants. It was later suggested by Sir Bernard Spilsbury that she may have been the victim of an abortion that went wrong.

THE TICHBORNE CLAIMANT

In 1854, Roger Tichborne, heir to the Tichborne baronetcy and fortune, went missing at sea off South America and was assumed drowned. His mother, Lady Tichborne, clung to the belief that he had survived and advertised in papers in Australia, hoping he had been shipwrecked there. In 1866 a man called Thomas Castro from Wagga Wagga, in Australia, claimed to be Tichborne. He travelled to England and was accepted by Lady Tichborne.

There was, however, growing evidence that Thomas Castro was actually Arthur Orton from Watford, who had gone missing in Australia some years before. A civil case from 1871 to 1872 rejected him as the claimant, and a criminal case against him began in 1873, lasting 188 days – making it one of the lengthiest heard in an English court. The case aroused huge popular interest. He was sentenced to fourteen years in jail and died in poverty in 1898.

▲ These small personal items were owned by Orton. The lock of Orton's hair was cut when he was in Millbank Prison.

One Penny — Pictorial Souvenir of the Great Tichborne Trial. 21 Portraits

▲ A small selection of the many pamphlets, broadsheets and cartoons that were produced to satisfy the public's insatiable appetite for news of the Tichborne case.

33

CAT BURGLAR AND MURDERER CHARLES PEACE

Charles Peace was born in Sheffield. He was a talented musician and in his teens he was known as 'The Modern Paganini'. He went on to become Britain's most successful cat burglar.

In August 1876 Peace shot and killed PC Cock in Manchester. He escaped, leaving a local man, William Habron, to be convicted. He returned to Sheffield where he shot dead his mistress's husband, Arthur Dyson. Once again he escaped, this time to London, and took up residence as a respectable gentleman with his wife and another woman, Susan Grey.

In October 1878 Peace was finally caught attempting to burgle a house in Blackheath. This time he shot the policeman but did not kill him. He was tried under his alias of John Ward and given a life sentence. Susan Grey later informed police of his real identity and he was returned to Yorkshire to stand trial for Arthur Dyson's murder. Peace was found guilty and was hanged on 25 February 1879 at Armley Prison. Before he was executed he confessed to PC Cock's murder and William Habron was given a free pardon.

Peace wrote two letters from his cell at Armley Prison on the day of his execution. One is addressed to the Vicar of Darnall, where Peace lived in Sheffield, and asks the people of the area to have pity on his family. The other letter is to 'My dear Friend' as 'A voice from the scaffold'. It confesses Peace's 'dreadful doings' and warns the recipient 'to give yourself to God'.

▲ This **hinged ladder** folds up, so Peace could carry it around at night unobtrusively. He would unfold it to gain access to upper-storey windows.

◄ **Thumb screw** which Charles Peace used for turning keys left in locks.

► This tiny **lantern** allowed Peace to work with minimum light and so avoid attention.

▼ Peace attached a hook to this **arm covering**, which concealed the fact that he was missing three fingers on one hand. Instead, he appeared to have no hand at all.

▲ Set of Peace's **lock picks**.

► Peace did not rely on other people to sell his stolen goods. He melted down jewellery himself in this **crucible**.

◄ **Wedge** used to secure the door of the room in which Peace was at work. He inserted a sharp tool through the hole in the wedge to fix it to the floor. In this way, he could prevent returning householders catching him unawares.

35

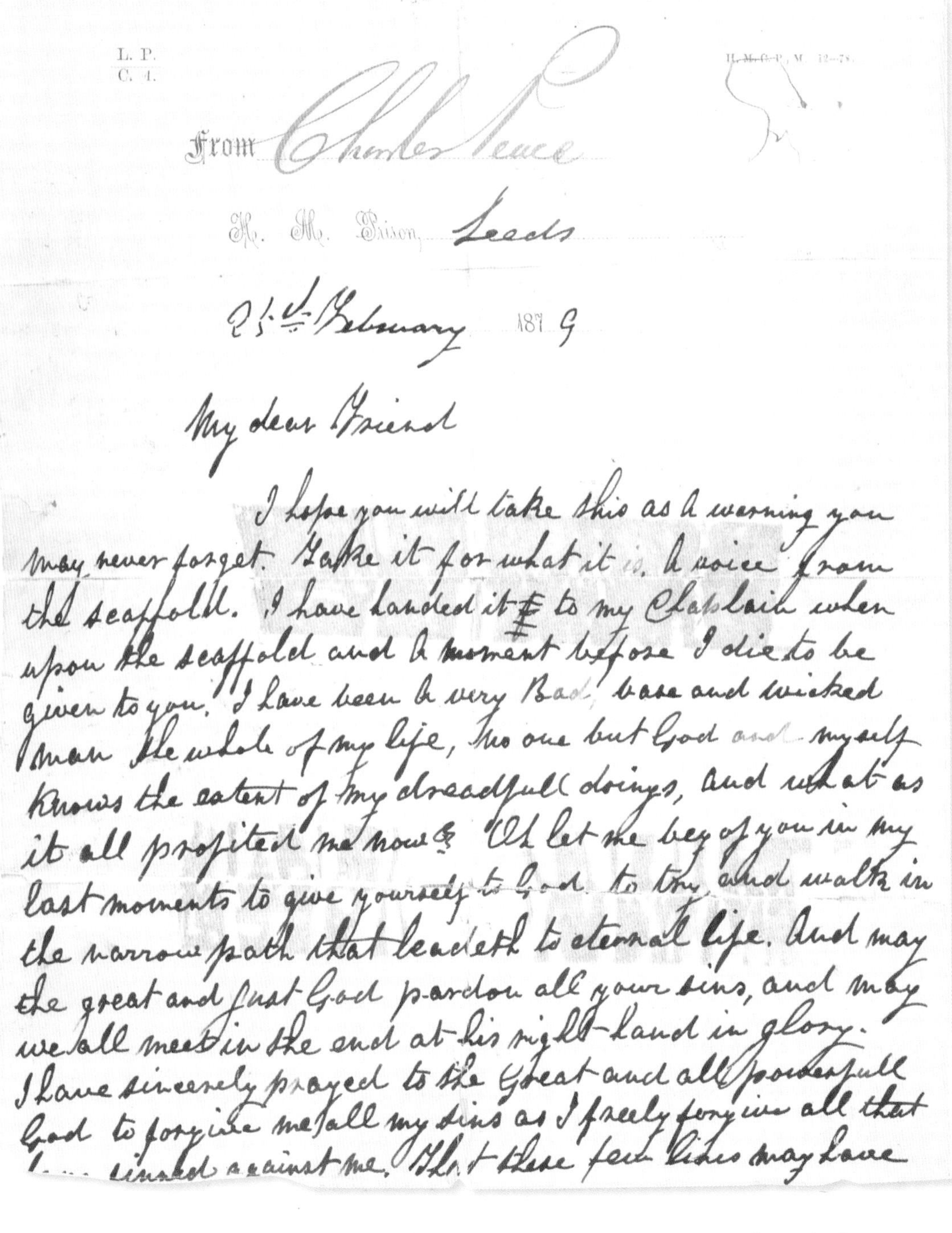

L. P.
C. I.

H. M. C. P. M. 12-78.

From Charles Peace

H. M. Prison, Leeds

25ᵗʰ February 187 9

My dear Friend

I hope you will take this as a warning you may never forget. Take it for what it is. A voice from the scaffold. I have handed it to my Chaplain when upon the scaffold and a moment before I die to be given to you. I have been a very Bad, base and wicked man the whole of my life, No one but God and myself knows the extent of my dreadfull doings, And what as it all profited me now? Oh let me beg of you in my last moments to give yourself to God. to try and walk in the narrow path that leadeth to eternal life. And may the great and Just God pardon all your sins, and may we all meet in the end at his right-hand in glory. I have sincerely prayed to the Great and all powerfull God to forgive me all my sins as I freely forgive all that ..... sinned against me. Oh, t these few lines may have

▲ **Letter from Charles Peace,**
25 February 1879.

MISCELLANEOUS ITEMS

CROWN AND ANCHOR GAME BOARD & DICE
late nineteenth century

This simple game was traditionally played for money by sailors. The dice are each marked with six symbols: crown, anchor, diamond, spade, club and heart. It was probably seized in connection with an illegal gambling venue.

ROULETTE WHEEL c.1885

This roulette wheel was seized at Barnet Fair in 1885. It has been adapted so that the operator can fix where the ball will land. A dent is visible in its outer ring which indicates to the operator where to fix the game. Barnet Fair was England's largest cattle market, with up to 40,000 animals sold over a few days. It was a haven for criminals: in 1874 *The Barnet Press* reported that 20 plainclothes detectives, 4 sergeants and 44 policemen had to be brought in. In 1888 there was an attempt to close it down as a public nuisance but it was saved by a petition from local businessmen.

KNIFE USED BY RICHARD PRINCE
to murder the actor William Terriss in 1897

William Terriss, 50, was a leading actor in late-nineteenth-century London. Richard Prince, 32, was also an actor, but much less successful. They were acquainted and Terriss helped Prince both to find work and financially. However, Prince became increasingly unstable and took against Terriss. On 16 December 1897 he waited outside the stage door of the Adelphi Theatre on Maiden Lane and stabbed Terriss to death as he arrived. He was found guilty, but 'according to the medical evidence, not responsible for his actions', and was sent to Broadmoor, where he died in 1936.

The Murderer of William Terriss

▲ **Drawing of Richard Prince** by William Hartley.

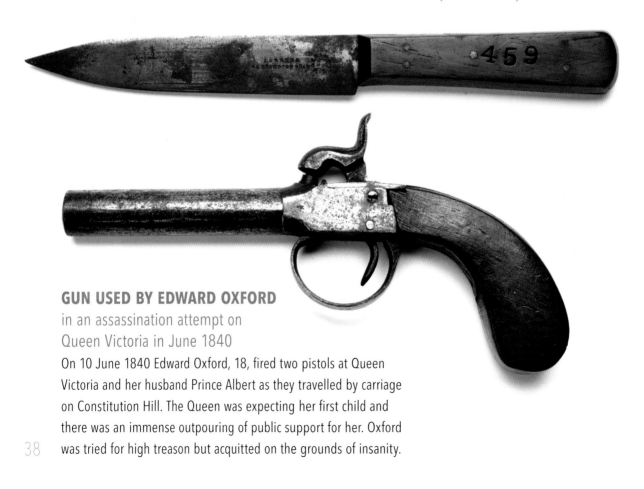

GUN USED BY EDWARD OXFORD
in an assassination attempt on Queen Victoria in June 1840

On 10 June 1840 Edward Oxford, 18, fired two pistols at Queen Victoria and her husband Prince Albert as they travelled by carriage on Constitution Hill. The Queen was expecting her first child and there was an immense outpouring of public support for her. Oxford was tried for high treason but acquitted on the grounds of insanity.

LACQUERED PAPIER MÂCHÉ SNUFF BOX
allegedly belonging to John Thurtell

In 1823 John Thurtell, 29, and two accomplices killed William Weare in Radlett, Hertfordshire. Thurtell owed Weare huge gambling debts but believed that Weare had cheated him. He shot Weare in the face, wounding him. As Weare tried to escape Thurtell cut his throat and beat him with the pistol, fracturing his skull. He and his accomplices then disposed of the body in a pond in Elstree. The weapons were left at the crime scene and inevitably they were traced back to Thurtell. The case received huge public attention. Thurtell was hanged outside Hertford Gaol on 9 January 1824. After his death his body was dissected for medical purposes.

Thurtell was supposedly a great taker of snuff and is alleged to have taken snuff from this box during his trial. This may be the snuff box referred to in an account of his trial and execution. When asked by the son of the governor of the prison for a memento, Thurtell said: 'Oh yes, I have got a snuff box, a plain one certainly, but I hope you will accept it for my sake'.

SAMPLER CUSHION
stitched by Annie Parker, 1879

Annie Parker appeared over 400 times before Greenwich Police Court on charges of drunkenness. She made this small sampler cushion, decorating it with hand-crocheted lace and embroidering it using her own hair instead of thread. She presented it to the Reverend Horsley, chaplain of the Clerkenwell House of Detention in 1879, and he gave it to the museum in 1884. Parker died of consumption in 1885, aged 35. At least two other examples of her work are known to exist.

WEAPONS COLLECTED BY CHARLES GRAHAM GRANT

Charles Graham Grant was a police surgeon in East London who also acted as a pathologist for the police. These four weapons were collected by him and have his visiting card attached with notes, giving his address as 523 Commercial Road. All these weapons were used in crimes in London between 1898 and the early 1900s.

KNUCKLEDUSTER

This knuckleduster was used in an assault and is labelled:

> Three blows ten wounds
> Bridge of nose broken and destroyed permanently?
> Sentence 3 months.

PEARL-HANDLED DOUBLE-BLADED PENKNIFE
used by a man to commit suicide, 1898

A man called Wilson went to stay at a friend's house. He borrowed this penknife from his host and later that night committed suicide, cutting his throat and stabbing himself. His lifeless body was found on a bed with one of his friend's young children asleep next to him. The jury at his inquest decided he was insane.

The original label attached to the penknife reads:

> 19 February 1898
> Found dead in bed with child (3 years old) sailor:
> vessels of neck cut through and stab in heart

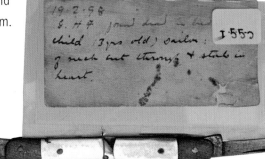

BONE-HANDLED DOUBLE-BLADED PENKNIFE
used by Thomas McDermott, 1900

Little is known about this object apart from what is written on the
original label, which reads:

> Cut throat
> Thomas McDermott
> 15.9.00 Discharged with caution

KNIFE used by Thomas Fairclough Barrow
to murder Emily Barrow, 1902

Emily Coates Barrow, 33, was stabbed to death with this knife
in Glamis Street, Shadwell, by her partner, Thomas Fairclough
Barrow, 49.

Thomas was Emily's stepfather; after her mother's death she lived
with him and they had two children. She was the main breadwinner;
according to the label, in the previous four years he had only worked
for one month. He was also abusive towards her and she had left him
about a week earlier.

On the morning of 18 October 1902 he followed her
as she walked to work and attacked her in the street.
He was hanged at Pentonville Prison
on 9 December 1902.

The original label reads:

> 18.10.02
> Th. Barrow killed Emily Barrow or Coates 26 his daughter?
> Who had borne him 2 children and kept him and them on
> 12/- per week. He did 1 month's work as night watchman
> in 4 years. Hanged

41

HANDCUFFS
c.1724 to late nineteenth century

These handcuffs were used to make arrests and restrain prisoners in London's police stations, courts and prisons. The pair labelled CM1/1 are reputed to have been worn by the notorious thief Jack Sheppard while he was in Newgate Prison. He famously escaped from Newgate four times but was eventually hanged at Tyburn on 16 November 1724 in front of a crowd of up to 200,000.

POLICE RECORDS

POLICE REPORT

Detective Inspector Glass wrote this report eighteen months after Police Constable George Cole was murdered in Dalston on 18 July 1882. On 6 October 1884 Thomas Orrock was hanged at Newgate Prison for the murder.

PC Cole had been shot by a man attempting to burgle a chapel in Dalston. A description of the suspect by witnesses led to Orrock, a petty thief. However, he was not picked out in an identity parade and was released.

Over a year later one of PC Cole's colleagues, PC Cobb, learned that Orrock had been practising shooting his gun on Tottenham marshes just before the murder. Cobb was taken to a tree there and found several bullets which matched those removed from PC Cole's body. Orrock, who was in Coldbath Prison for another crime, was arrested for PC Cole's murder. This four-page report records DI Glass's investigation between February and June 1884.

This case involved what was probably the earliest recorded use of ballistics evidence by the Metropolitan Police.

PRISONERS' ANTHROPOMETRIC RECORD CARDS
late nineteenth century

Under the Prevention of Crimes Act 1871, Scotland Yard held a central register of prisoners nationwide who were sentenced to imprisonment for a month or more. Prison governors were required to send details on cards to the Metropolitan Police. These are a selection of such cards in the Crime Museum's collections.

The *Illustrated London News* of 29 September 1883 contains a description of how prisoners' photographs should be taken:

> The photograph … should be taken as near the convict's or prisoner's liberation as possible, and in ordinary dress; and the face should be placed in half profile, so that the shape of the nose may appear … the men hold up their hands so as to be shown in their photographs … finding their shape and conditions extremely significant.

44

ANTHROPOMETRIC MEASURING CALLIPERS
late nineteenth century

From 1894 to 1901 the Metropolitan Police used both Alphonse Bertillon's anthropometric system and fingerprinting to record details of convicted prisoners. In 1901 its Anthropometric Department was replaced by the Fingerprint Bureau.

In addition to recording physical details such as hair and eye colour, height and complexion, anthropometry measured head length and breadth, face breadth, mid-left finger, left foot and left cubit (forearm). These callipers were used for measuring these body parts.

COURTROOM ILLUSTRATIONS BY WILLIAM HARTLEY

William Hartley (1862–1937) was a leading courtroom artist whose work appeared in many of the leading newspapers of the time. Six volumes of his original courtroom sketches were donated to the Crime Museum; they cover the period 1893 to 1918. The sketches are in pen-and-ink or pencil.

GEORGE CHAPMAN,
aka Severin Klosowski, 'The Borough Poisoner'

George Chapman (below) was born in Poland, where he undertook basic medical training. He moved to London in his twenties and went into business, eventually running a barbershop and two public houses. He married and had two children but subsequently took up with a number of other women, three of whom he poisoned. The last of these was Maud Marsh (above), who was living with him as his wife when she died on 22 October 1902. A post-mortem showed she had died of antimony poisoning. The bodies of two of his previous partners, Isabella Spink and Elizabeth Taylor, were exhumed and traces of poison were again found. He was convicted of the murder of Maud Marsh and hanged at Wandsworth Prison on 7 April 1903. Chapman is one of the people who have been identified as possibly being Jack the Ripper.

ALFRED J. MONSON
at his trial for fraud in 1898

In 1893 Monson was accused of the murder of his pupil, the wealthy Cecil Hambrough, in a shooting accident on the Ardlamont Estate in Argyllshire, Scotland. The case was found 'not proven' in Scottish law. Two years later he won a libel case against Madame Tussaud's for displaying a waxwork of him, but was awarded only a farthing in damages. In 1898 he was accused of defrauding the Norwich Union Life Assurance Society at Bow Street and sentenced to five years' imprisonment with hard labour.

· MONSON IN COURT ·

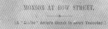

MONSON AT BOW STREET.

· MR ROSS DESCRIBES THE ATTACK ·

THE PRISONER FACES THE COURT

JOHANN SCHNEIDER
the St Pancras Oven Murder

In 1898 Johann Schneider, 36, killed Conrad Berndt, 19, a baker's assistant, and put his body into the bakery oven. He then attempted to kill the baker, William Ross. Schneider had worked previously for Ross as his assistant but had been out of work for some time and unable to support his wife and children. He was hanged at Newgate Prison on 3 January 1899.

CHARLES WELLS
at his trial for fraud in 1893

Charles Wells was a gambler and swindler who may well have been
the inspiration for the 1892 song 'The Man Who Broke the Bank
at Monte Carlo'. Wells persuaded people in Britain to invest in his
bogus inventions. He then took the money and travelled to Monte
Carlo to gamble. He broke the bank at the Casino de Monte Carlo
a number of times in 1891 and 1892.

Breaking the bank means winning more
money than is available at a table in the
casino. The Casino hired detectives to
try to catch him out, but they never succeeded. However, in 1892, he also lost,
including the money he had defrauded
from his investors. He was extradited to
Britain and sentenced at the Old Bailey
to eight years in prison.

PROFESSOR AND MADAME KEIRO

Charles and Martha Stephenson, known as Professor and Madame
Keiro, were palmists or fortune-tellers who stood trial in 1904 with
Charles Fricker, known as Yoga, a crystal-gazer. They operated in the
West End. The case against them was brought at the instigation of
Sir Alfred Harmsworth, owner of the *Daily Mail*. He wanted to ensure
that West End fortune-tellers with wealthy patrons were dealt with
in the same way as Gypsy fortune-tellers at rural fairs, who were
regularly prosecuted. The Keiros and Yoga were found guilty of attempting to obtain money by false pretences and of fortune-telling.
As this was seen as a test case, they were only fined, but were
warned that if they were caught again they would be imprisoned.

Mr WIELAND TELLS HOW HE SAW THE BLOWS STRUCK

MR JUSTICE DARLING WRITES DOWN THE EVIDENCE

LOCKIE WHO GAVE THE PRISONER INTO CUSTODY

MR BAKER STATES

THAT DECEASED WAS HIS BROTHER

MISS BYRON IN THE DOCK ATTENDED BY A WARDRESS

ROBT COLEMAN WHO TOOK THE MESSAGE TO MR BAKER

EMMA 'KITTY' BYRON

Kitty Byron was 24 and living with her older lover, Reginald Baker, 44, a stockbroker. He was often drunk and violent. On 7 November they argued so much that their landlady asked them to move out. Baker replied that Byron would return to live with her mother. Byron bought a knife and went to the post office on Lombard Street.
She sent a messenger to get Baker from the Stock Exchange. They argued in the street outside and then she stabbed him, killing him. She was found guilty, with the jury making a strong recommendation for mercy. Following a public petition, her death sentence was commuted to life imprisonment. She was released in 1908.

ELIZABETH CAMP

Elizabeth Camp, 33, was murdered on 11 February 1897 while travelling on a train between Walworth, where she was visiting relatives, and London Waterloo. Her fiancé was waiting for her at Waterloo and identified her body.

In 1906 a soldier, Robert Clive, alias James Thornton, falsely confessed to the murder. He was charged and appeared at Westminster Police Court, where the charges were dropped. This image of Camp was produced by Hartley at the time of the 1906 case. Her murderer was never found.

AMELIA SACH AND ANNIE WALTERS
'the Finchley Baby Farmers'

Amelia Sach and Annie Walters were 'baby farmers' in Finchley, North London. Sach had a lying-in home where women could go to give birth, and soon she also advertised that she would keep the babies afterwards, or would take in other unwanted children, for a fee. This was mainly aimed at poor unmarried women who had little option but to give their child up for adoption. Annie Walters worked for Sach and would collect and later poison the child. It is not known how many children they killed. They were finally caught when Walter's landlord, a police officer, grew suspicious of her. They were hanged at Holloway Prison on 3 February 1903, the last female double execution in Britain.

LOUISE MASSETT

This image shows Louise Massett, 33, while on trial for the murder of her 3-year-old son, Manfred. She was found guilty and hanged at Newgate Prison on 9 January 1900. Manfred was her illegitimate son, who had been fostered by a Mrs Gentle since he was a small baby. She told Gentle that she was taking him to live with his father in France, but Manfred's body, wrapped only in a shawl, was found in the toilets at Dalston Junction station. He had been beaten and smothered.

WILLIAM JOHNSON ('HARRY THE VALET') AND MOSS LIPMAN

On 17 October 1898 the Dowager Duchess of Sutherland's jewels were stolen at the Gard du Nord, Paris. A month later Johnson (also known as Henry Williams or 'Harry the Valet') and Moss Lipman were arrested and charged. Some of the jewels were found at the address where the arrests were made.

Charges against Lipman were subsequently dropped. Johnson was sentenced to seven years' imprisonment with hard labour. Only about £4,000 of the estimated £30,000 of jewellery was ever recovered. The sketch also shows Detective Inspector Froest, who was later involved in the Crippen investigation.

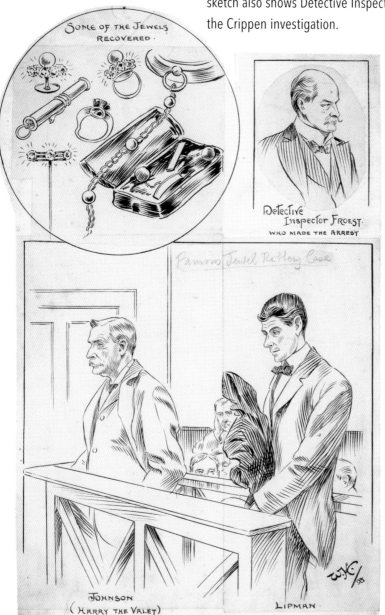

SOME OF THE JEWELS RECOVERED.

Detective Inspector FROEST.
WHO MADE THE ARREST

JOHNSON
(HARRY THE VALET)

LIPMAN.

THE CRIME MUSEUM 1905 TO TODAY

Over the past century London has expanded and its population has become more diverse. Londoners' lives have been transformed and social customs and attitudes have altered greatly. Crime, detection and punishment in the capital have also developed and become increasingly complex.

The museum's collections reflect this story of change. At the same time they reveal how crimes such as murder, robbery, rape and terrorism have been repeated and how motives such as greed, sex, jealousy and political beliefs have reappeared. They also shed light on the work of detectives, scientists, pathologists and photographers, and on new methods of investigation.

The following sections address a number of criminal cases individually and explore themes within the collections. All were well known in their time and many remain notorious today. Behind them are real people, each with their own story. All affected the lives of the victims and their families and friends.

CURATORS

Until 1954, when its first full-time civilian curator was appointed, serving police officers showed visitors around the museum. From 1955 onwards, its curators have been retired officers.

1954	Alexander Hannay
1955	George Somerset
1957	Charles Dawson
1970	James Mackle
1976	Thomas McMacken
1981	William Waddell
1993	John Ross
2005	Alan McCormick
2011	Dave Thompson
2012	Paul Bickley

INDIVIDUAL CASES

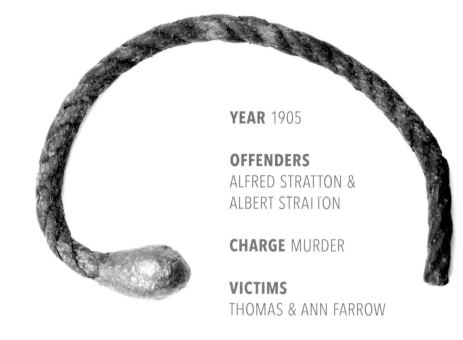

YEAR 1905

OFFENDERS
ALFRED STRATTON &
ALBERT STRATTON

CHARGE MURDER

VICTIMS
THOMAS & ANN FARROW

When William Jones arrived for work on Monday, 27 March 1905 at Chapman's Oil & Colour Stores in Deptford High Street, he found the body of his elderly manager, Thomas Farrow, lying in the shop parlour. Mr Farrow, who had worked for Chapman's for many years, had been badly beaten. His 65-year-old wife, Ann, lay dying in bed upstairs. Detectives discovered three stocking masks and an empty cash box at the crime scene. The cash box had contained the previous week's takings. In early April Alfred and Albert Stratton, two local brothers in their early twenties, were arrested.

At Alfred and Albert's trial in May, witnesses confirmed they had seen two men matching the brothers' descriptions leave the shop around the time of the murders. Other witnesses said they had met Alfred with his brother in the area shortly before then. Alfred's girlfriend, Hannah Cromarty, testified that she had slept all night unaware of his whereabouts but that in the morning he had smelled of paraffin. Most damning, however, was evidence from Detective Inspector Charles Collins of Scotland Yard's Fingerprint Department that a thumbprint found on the empty cash box corresponded to Alfred's right thumb.

The jury found Alfred and Albert Stratton guilty of murder and on Tuesday 23 May 1905 they were hanged together at Wandsworth Prison. This was the first criminal case in British history where fingerprint evidence secured a conviction for murder.

▲ **Cosh.** Dudley Burnie, the police surgeon who conducted the post-mortem on Mr Farrow, confirmed that a heavy blunt instrument had caused his injuries. He noted that one wound had been made by an instrument that was 'not straight'.

▼ **Courtroom sketch**, 5 May 1905, by William Hartley, showing Alfred and Albert Stratton sitting in the dock at the Old Bailey on the third day of their trial. The next day they were both found guilty of murder and sentenced to death.

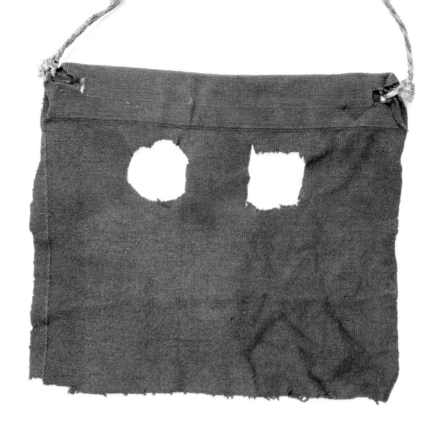

THE STRATTON BROTHERS

► Witness evidence helped link the brothers to three **stocking masks** which were found at the crime scene. One witness testified that Alfred once asked her for stockings whilst another recalled she had found stocking masks under Albert's mattress.

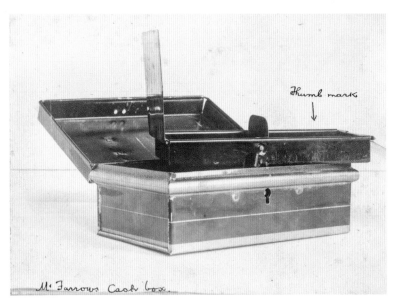

◀ **Cash box** found at the crime scene, 1905.

▼ Enlarged photograph of **thumbprint**, 1905.

▼ **Police fingerprint evidence register**. The first entry on this page refers to the cash-box thumbprint which led to the brothers' conviction. At their trial DI Collins explained in detail how it corresponded to Alfred's right thumb.

Nº	Date	Place	Sentence	Name	Article	Address	Ref to C2D File	Remarks
16	6. 5. 05	C.C.C.	Death	Alfred Stratton	Cash Box	Mr & Mrs Farrow High St. Deptford		Deptford Mask Murder
17	15. 7. 05	Kent Assizes	3 yrs P.S.	M Jas McAllister	Ginger beer bottle	"P" Div Bromley	1616/62	Pleaded guilty Other evidence
18	24. 05	Salisbury Assizes	12 mos H.L.	Alfd Bowman	Piece of Glass	Amesbury	405.03	
19	17. 10. 05	Lewes Dn Sess	18 mos H.L.	Chas H. Gauntlett	Marks on Fanlight	Eastbourne		
20	8. 11. 05	Them Dn Sess	6 mos H.L.	Dennis Kennedy	Window Glass	Birmingham "The Britannia" P.H.	296/02	Pleaded not guilty
21	2. 1. 06	Leeds W.R.Sess	9 "	S Stanley Barker	Window Glass	Halifax	3132/05	DI Emy 26.12.05
22	10. Apl. 06	Hastings Police Ct	6 wks	Otto Scherf	Electric lamp	Hastings	228 F.P.	Pleaded not guilty at two hearings of this case but plea did guilty after 3 period evidence
23	3. 8. 06	West Ham Boro Sess	3 yrs P.S.	Wm Reed	Piece of Glass	1 Wilberforce Ct Canning Town K	10/06	Pleaded guilty at the last moment at Sessions
24	23. 10. 06	N. L. Sess	2 years H.L.	Wm Brown 4485	piece of glass	23 Orchard Plan Blackwall	6185	Plead not guilty Found guilty No other evidence
25	26. 11. 06	Lewes Sess	18 mos	J Ferguson	Fanlight	Eastbourne	F.P. 50/24	No other evidence

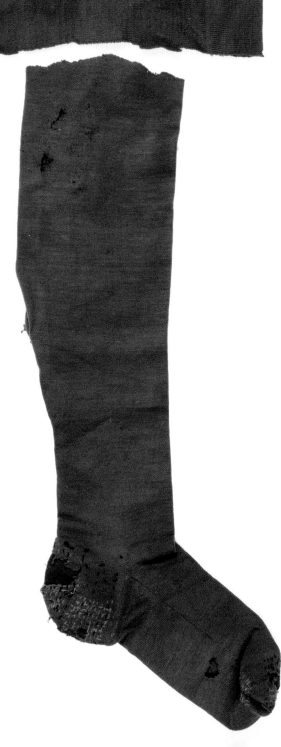

▼ **Chapman's Oil & Colour Stores**, Deptford High Street, 1905.

▶ This **stocking**, which has its top cut off, was found by Sergeant Atkinson in a bundle of clothing in the shop parlour. Its cut edge fits one of the masks precisely.

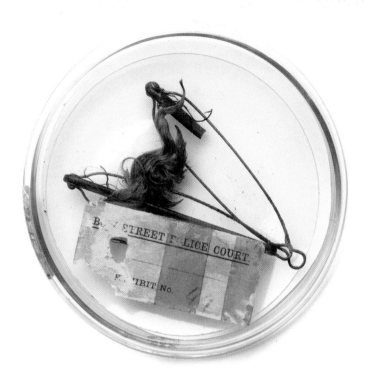

YEAR 1910

OFFENDER
DR HAWLEY HARVEY
CRIPPEN

CHARGE MURDER

VICTIM
CORA CRIPPEN

▲ **Hair samples and curlers**
found buried with Cora's remains.
Her friends Adeline Harrison and
Clara Martinetti testified that the
samples matched Cora's hair,
which she used to dye auburn.

◄ **Cora Crippen,** also known
by her professional name Belle
Elmore.

The last time Cora Crippen's friends, the Martinettis, saw her alive
was for supper on 31 January 1910 at the Crippens' home in
Hilldrop Crescent, Holloway. Two days later Dr Crippen's mistress,
Ethel Le Neve, delivered a note from Cora to the Music Hall Ladies'
Guild resigning as its treasurer. Written in Crippen's hand, it claimed
Cora had been called away to America. In March Crippen told her
friends she was ill and then that she had died. By early July Cora's
friends were suspicious enough to go to Scotland Yard. Cora, a
music-hall singer, was 35 years old.

When Inspector Walter Dew questioned Crippen he admitted
inventing Cora's death to cover his humiliation at her leaving him
for another man. Satisfied with this explanation, Dew left. But when
he visited Crippen's office three days later, the doctor and Le Neve
had disappeared. Crippen's house was searched and human remains
discovered. An international appeal for the fugitives resulted in a
ship's captain telegraphing Scotland Yard from his vessel to report his
suspicions about two passengers. Dew boarded a faster ship, and on
31 July arrested Crippen and Le Neve in Quebec.

Crippen was found guilty of murdering Cora. Insisting on Le
Neve's innocence until the end, he was hanged at Pentonville Prison
on Wednesday, 23 November 1910. This was the first time a ship's
wireless technology had been used to help catch a suspect.

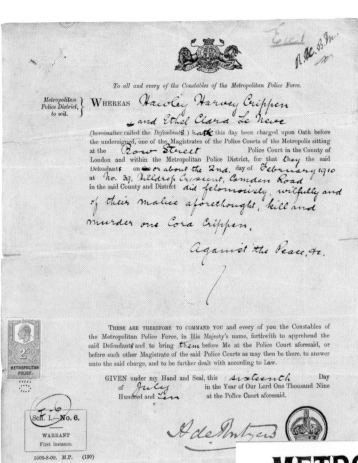

► These **pyjama fragments** were wrapped around Cora's remains. Crippen argued that the body must have been buried before he and Cora moved into their house in 1905. However, the pyjama label reads 'Jones Brothers (Holloway), Limited'. The store only became a limited company in 1906.

► This **spade** was used by Dr Crippen to bury Cora's remains. Pathologist Sir Bernard Spilsbury, in his first widely publicised case, identified the remains as Cora's by demonstrating that a scar on abdominal tissue matched an operation Cora had undergone.

► **Police officers digging** at 39 Hilldrop Crescent, Holloway, 1910.

▲ **Arrest warrant**, 16 July 1910. The discovery of Cora's remains and Crippen's and Le Neve's disappearance provided enough evidence to issue this arrest warrant.

► **Appeal poster**, 16 July 1910. *SS Montrose*'s captain Henry Kendall's telegram to Scotland Yard read 'Have strong suspicions that Crippen – London cellar murderer and accomplice are among Saloon passengers. Moustache taken off – growing beard. Accomplice dressed as boy. Voice manner and build undoubtedly a girl.'

▶ **Dr Crippen and Ethel Le Neve**, 1910, by William Hartley. Crippen and Le Neve had met in about 1901 at Drouet's Institute for the Deaf, where she was a typist and he was a consulting specialist.

▼ **Telegram**, 31 July 1910. On 31 July Dew boarded the SS *Montrose* on her arrival at Father Point, Quebec. He sent this telegram to Scotland Yard confirming Crippen's and Le Neve's arrest. 'Handcuffs London' was Scotland Yard's telegraphic address.

BOW STREET

THE WESTERN UNION TELEGRAPH COMPANY.
THE LARGEST TELEGRAPHIC SYSTEM IN EXISTENCE.
DIRECT ROUTE FOR ALL PARTS OF THE UNITED STATES, CANADA, CENTRAL AMERICA, WEST INDIES, SOUTH AMERICA, & VIA THE PACIFIC CABLE TO AUSTRALIA, NEW ZEALAND, FANNING, FIJI AND NORFOLK ISLANDS.

ATLANTIC CABLES direct to CANADA and to NEW YORK CITY.
DIRECT WIRES TO ALL THE PRINCIPAL CITIES.

To   *Handcuffs Ldn Eng*

Crippen and Leneve arrested wire later Dew

The public are requested to hand in their replies at the Company's Stations, where free receipts are given for the amounts charged.
CABLE ADDRESSES ARE REGISTERED FREE OF CHARGE.
No inquiry respecting this Message can be attended to without the production of this Paper.

▶ **Courtroom sketches**, 1910, by William Hartley. Crippen and Le Neve travelled on the SS *Montrose* disguised as John Robinson and his son. William Long, with whom Crippen had worked, testified that Crippen had asked him to buy boys' clothes.

▶ **Trial exhibit labels**, marked 'Messrs. Attenborough / Contract Notes / Exhibits 24 & 27'. In February 1910 Crippen visited Attenborough's pawnbrokers in Oxford Street to pawn diamond jewellery later identified as Cora's.

▶ **Full Account of the Crippen Horror**, c.1910. Cora's murder sparked massive public excitement. This booklet's cover captures at a glance the elements in the case which fascinated the public: a music-hall singer, a twice-married man, a quack 'doctor' and the thrill of new technology.

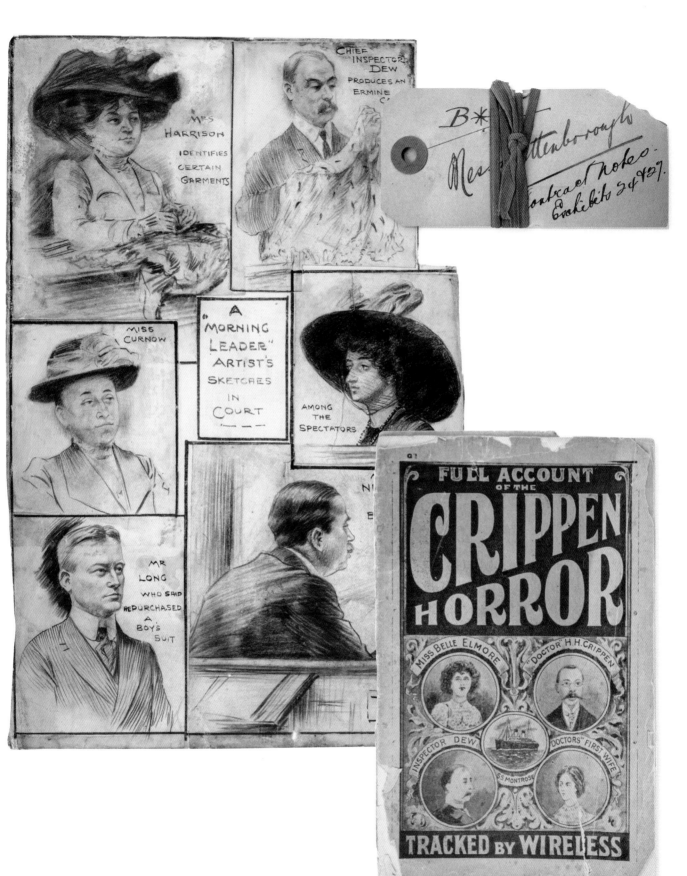

On the night of 16 December 1910 five unarmed City of London Police officers were shot when they were called to an attempted burglary by a group of Latvian revolutionaries at a jeweller's shop in Houndsditch. Sergeants Robert Bentley and Charles Tucker and Constable Walter Choate died. Sergeant Bryant and Constable Ernest Woodhams were seriously injured. The gang escaped but after an intensive search some members were arrested and later stood trial.

Two weeks after the shootings the police learned that some gang members were hiding in a flat at 100 Sidney Street, Stepney. On 3 January 1911, 200 armed City of London and Metropolitan Police officers surrounded the house. Aware that the gang had superior guns and were well positioned, the officers requested military help from the Scots Guards, who were stationed nearby. The besieged men fired from windows while police and troops shot back. The Home Secretary, Winston Churchill, arrived, followed by artillery guns. The house eventually caught fire and the bodies of two gang members were found in the ruins. An injured fireman, Charles Pearson, died afterwards in hospital.

The Siege of Sidney Street was the first time in London's history that the police had requested military assistance to deal with an armed siege. It was also the first siege to be recorded on film. Criticism of the police's ineffective weapons led to modern guns being introduced.

YEAR 1911

▶ **Mauser C96 pistol**, found in the Sidney Street ruins. It was one of several modern semi-automatic guns used by the gang. The weapons available to the Metropolitan Police were old-fashioned Webley revolvers that had first been supplied in 1884.

▼ **Postcards**, 1911. Crowds flocked to watch the siege, which soon attracted the name 'The Battle of Stepney'. The gunfight was captured on film, and souvenirs and postcards quickly appeared. These postcards follow events as they unfolded during the day.

THE SIEGE OF SIDNEY STREET

EAST END SIEGE. — Maxim gun ready for action.

No 2. The Burning House in Sidney St. where Assassins Perished.

◀ **Courtroom sketches** by William Hartley. In April 1911 Zurka Dubof, Jacob Peters, John Rosen and Nina Vassileva, all in their twenties, were tried in connection with the Houndsditch murders and attempted robbery. The men were acquitted and Vassileva's conviction was quashed on appeal.

▶ Detective Inspector John Mulvaney is shown at the trial holding a Mauser C96 pistol found in the ruins of 100 Sidney Street. He played a key role in the joint City of London and Metropolitan Police siege.

▼ **Postcards** of the siege.

EAST END SIEGE. — After the battle: Firemen extinguishing the flames, and Scots Guards assembled.

▶ **Posters**, 22 December 1910. These posters appeal for information about members of the Houndsditch gang. They feature one member, George Gardstein, who was accidentally shot as he escaped. He died the next day. The Russian translation was aimed at the East End's large Russian community.

▼ **Memorandum**, 25 January 1911, giving police officers a description of Peter Piatkow, a Latvian artist and scene painter at the Jubilee Street Anarchist Club. The police believed he might be the Houndsditch gang's leader.

CITY OF LONDON POLICE.
MURDER OF POLICE OFFICERS.
£500 REWARD

WHEREAS Sergeants Charles Tucker and Robert Bentley, and Constable Walter Charles Choat, of the City of London Police, were murdered in Exchange Buildings, in the said City, at 11.30 p.m., on the 16th December, 1910, by a man who is now dead, and other persons now wanted, whose descriptions are given below, and who were also concerned with the deceased Murderer in attempting to feloniously break and enter a Jeweller's shop, and killed the Officers to prevent arrest.

PORTRAIT AND DESCRIPTION OF THE DEAD MURDERER.

Name said to be GEORGE GARDSTEIN, alias POOLKA MILOWITZ.

Both may be incorrect.

DESCRIPTION :
Age about 24, height 5ft. 9 in., complexion pale, hair brown, slight dark moustache worn slightly up at ends, good physique.

DESCRIPTION OF THE PERSONS WANTED.

FIRST.—A man named FRITZ SVARRS, lately residing at 69, Grove Street, Commercial Road, London, E., age about 24 or 25, height 5 feet 8 or 9 inches, complexion sallow, hair fair, medium moustache—turned up at ends, lighter in colour than hair of head, eyes grey, nose rather small, slightly turned up, chin a little upraised, has a few [...] slightly forward ; dress brown tweed [...] usually wears a grey Irish tweed cap [...] native of Libau, Russia.

[...] at 59, Grove Street, Commercial Road, [...] and medium moustache black, clear [...] (broad dark stripes), black overcoat [...] believed to be a native [...] Russia.

[...] full breasts, complexion medium, face [...] and skirt, white blouse, large black hat

[...] for the City of London to any person [...] or in proportion to the number of such [...] London, E.C., or at any Police Station.

NOTT BOWER,
Commissioner of Police for the City of London.

ЛОНДОНСКАЯ ПОЛ...
(СИТИ).
УБІЙСТВО ПОЛИЦЕЙСКИХЪ ЧИНОВЪ.
НАГРАДА £500

16-го Декабря 1910 года, въ 11 ч. 30 м. ночи, въ Эксчейнжъ Бьлдингъ, находящейся въ Сити, были убиты злоумышленникомъ, который теперь мертъ, сержанты полиціи ЧАРЛЬЗЪ ТАКЕРЪ, РОБЕРТЪ БЕНТЛИ, и полисменъ ВАЛЬТЕРЪ ЧАРЛЬЗЪ ЧОУТЪ. Другія лица, совмѣстно съ умершимъ убійцей пытавшіяся взломать и забраться въ ювелирный магазинъ, стрѣлявшія и убившія полицейскихъ чиновъ для того чтобы избѣжать ареста, подробное описаніе примѣтъ которыхъ дано ниже, теперь ищутся полиціей.

Фотографія и примѣты умершаго убійцы.

Имена (предполагаютъ):

ГЕОРГЪ ГАРДШТЕЙНЪ или же ПУЛКА МИЛОВИЧЪ.

Оба имени могутъ быть не точны.

ПРИМѢТЫ:
Около 24 лѣтъ отъ роду, ростъ 5 фут. 9 дюйм., наружность блѣдная, волоса темно-русыя, маленькія темноватыя усы заверченныя кверху, крѣпкаго тѣлосложенія.

Описанія примѣтъ скрывшихся лицъ.

1.—Человѣкъ, извѣстный подъ названіемъ ФРИТЦЪ СВАРРСЪ, жившій на 59, Гроувъ-Стритъ, Коммершель Роудъ, Лондонъ. Лѣтъ, около 24-хъ лѣтъ отъ роду, ростъ 5 фут. 8 дюймовъ, наружность блѣдная, волоса свѣтлые, усы средней величины, завороченные кверху, свѣтлѣе чѣмъ волоса на головѣ; глаза сѣрые, носъ малъ, слегка загнутый кверху, подбородокъ выдающійся, имѣетъ нѣсколько маленькихъ угрей на лицѣ, сухы выдающіяся, плечи ровныя, слегка выдающіяся впередъ; костюмъ коричневаго ивѣта (съ тонкой свѣтлой полоской), темное касторовое пальто (бархатный воротникъ, почти возлѣ) обыкновенно носитъ сѣрую шапку ирландской матеріи (съ краснымъ волосомъ), его также видѣли въ мягкой шляпѣ. „Гриль." слесарь; уроженецъ Либау, Россіи.

2.—Человѣкъ, извѣстный подъ названіемъ „ПИТЕРЪ ДИ ПЕЙПТЕРЪ," жившій на 59, Гроувъ Стритъ, Коммершель Роудъ. Лѣтъ, 28-30 лѣтъ отъ роду, ростъ 5 футовъ 9 или 10 дюймовъ, наружность блѣдная, волоса и усы (средней вел.) — черные, чистая кожа, глаза черные, средняго тѣлосложенія, на видъ осторожный; костюмъ коричневаго цвѣта (широкая полоска), черное пальто (бархатный воротникъ, пополированный), носитъ черную твердую касторовую шляпу, черныя ботинки на шнуркахъ, видъ небрежный. Предполагаютъ что онъ русскій подданный.

3.—Женщина, 26 или 30 лѣтъ; ростъ 5 фут. 4 дюйма, тѣлосложеніе худое, нѣсколько полноватая въ груди, наружность средняя, лицо нѣжнаго очертанія, глаза сѣрые, волоса темнорусые; имѣетъ три четверти длины и юбки темнаго цвѣта, бѣлая блузка, большая черная шляпа (отдѣланная чернымъ шелкомъ), свѣтло-шейныя ботинки.

Вышеупомянутая награда будетъ выдана полицеймейстеромъ Сити, полностью или по частямъ, согласно числу лицъ арестованныхъ, тѣмъ лицамъ, которыя доставятъ необходимыя свѣдѣнія могущія способствовать къ аресту злоумышленныхъ лицъ.

Со всѣми свѣдѣніями просятъ обращаться въ Полицейское Управленіе Сити, 26, Олдъ Джури, или въ какое либо другое полицейское училище.

City Police Office,
26, Old Jewry, London, E.C.

J. W. NOTT BOWER,
Полицеймейстеръ Лондонскаго Сити.

Metropolitan Police Office.

510

JANUARY 25TH, 1911.

SPECIAL MEMORANDUM.

WANTED FOR CRIME

CP (6) Peter Piatkow, alias Schtern, and "Peter the Painter" (7 [...]ber). 19th December last) a Russian, late of 59, Grove-street, Commercial-road, E., 28 to 30, 5ft 9 to 10, complexion sallow, hair and medium moustache black, clear sharp, clear skin, eyes dark, medium build, reserved manner. For being concerned with others in the murder of three police officers and attempting to break into a jeweller's shop on 16th December, 1910.

In July 1910 Miss Eliza Barrow, 47, and Ernest Grant, the young boy she looked after, began lodging with insurance superintendent Frederick Seddon, 40, his wife Margaret, 34, and their four children at 63 Tollington Park, Holloway. Just over a year later Miss Barrow became unwell. A local doctor visited and prescribed medicine but two weeks later she was dead.

When Miss Barrow's cousin, Frank Vonderahe, heard of her death, he visited the Seddons. He learned that, although she had a family vault, Seddon had arranged for her burial in a common grave. He also discovered that since 1910 she had transferred all her property and stocks to Seddon in return for a monthly income and free accommodation. Finally, under a will written during her final illness and witnessed by members of the Seddon family, Seddon became her sole executor. Vonderahe went straight to the police.

When Miss Barrow's body was examined, arsenic was found. Mr and Mrs Seddon were arrested and tried. Seddon alone was found guilty of poisoning Miss Barrow with arsenic extracted from flypapers. The evidence against him was inconsistent and a petition requesting a reprieve was signed by 100,000 people. It was unsuccessful and he was hanged at Pentonville Prison on Thursday, 18 April 1912.

The signatures of Frederick Seddon and William Seddon (almost certainly his father) appear in the Crime Museum's visitors' book on 1 December 1905. It is not known why they visited.

YEAR 1912

OFFENDERS
FREDERICK SEDDON &
MARGARET SEDDON

CHARGE MURDER

VICTIM ELIZA BARROW

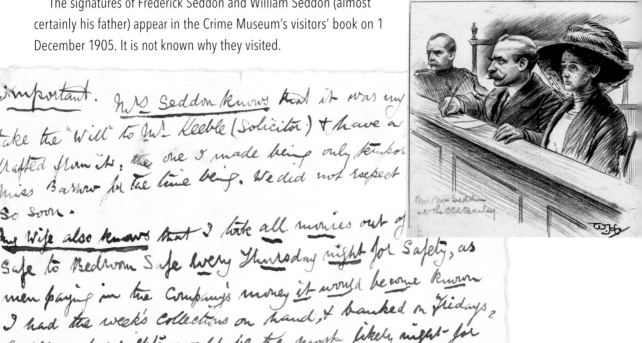

THE SEDDONS

◄ **Mather's arsenical flypaper.**
Evidence at the trial revolved around the flypapers in Miss Barrow's room during her illness. The prosecution contended that Miss Barrow had been poisoned with arsenic extracted from them.

◄ **Marsh's mirror test.** Senior Home Office scientific analyst Henry Willcox used this equipment to test Miss Barrow's kidney for arsenic. The black deposit (called a 'mirror') visible in the tube confirmed its presence.

▲ **Experiment bottles** containing the results of Willcox's experiments to extract arsenic from flypapers and mix it with Valentine's Meat Juice and brandy, which Miss Barrow's doctor had prescribed. The prosecution argued that this was how the Seddons administered the arsenic.

◄ **Miss Eliza Barrow.**

◄ Courtroom sketch by William Hartley showing **Mr and Mrs Seddon** sitting in the dock at the Old Bailey. Mr Seddon is making notes.

◄ **Notes** written by Frederick Seddon during his trial or his appeal hearing.

69

YEAR 1918

CHARGE MURDER

OFFENDER
DAVID GREENWOOD

VICTIM NELLIE TREW

On the evening of 9 February 1918, 16-year-old Nellie Trew went to visit Plumstead Library. The following morning her body was discovered on Eltham Common. She had been raped and strangled. Close by were a button attached to a piece of wire and a military badge from the Leicestershire Regiment.

Chief Inspector Francis Carlin of Scotland Yard arranged for images of the button and badge to appear in the press. David Greenwood was a 21-year-old metal turner who had served with the Leicestershire Regiment in the war. A workmate of his recognised the badge as similar to one that Greenwood regularly wore. When challenged, Greenwood said he had sold it to a man he met on a tram. Greenwood made a statement to police. When Carlin met him he noticed Greenwood's coat was missing buttons and identified the button as coming from it. Furthermore, the wire was identified as coming from the factory where Greenwood worked.

Greenwood denied having ever met Nellie but was found guilty and sentenced to death. This was changed to life imprisonment after an appeal. He was released in 1933 at the age of 36.

But was Greenwood guilty? He had been discharged from the army due to a weak heart and fainting fits, having been buried alive in a trench in 1917. At his trial it was suggested he would have been too weak to kill Nellie. Three years after the crime, Albert Lytton, who was by then in a psychiatric hospital, admitted to having killed Nellie, but his claims were dismissed.

▶ Police photographs of **David Greenwood** on his arrest in 1918, and on his release in 1933.

▲ **Coat button**, one of the two items that led to the conviction of Greenwood. The original piece of wire is still looped through the button. It is shown with its original Woolwich Police Court evidence label.

▶ The other object that convicted Greenwood is this **military badge** in the form of a tiger, the emblem of the Leicestershire Regiment. It is shown with its original Woolwich Police Court evidence label.

DAVID GREENWOOD

BYWATERS
& THOMPSON

YEAR 1922

CHARGE MURDER

OFFENDERS
FREDERICK BYWATERS
& EDITH THOMPSON

VICTIM
PERCY THOMPSON

▲ Percy Thompson was stabbed with this **knife**. Edith was heard calling out to the attacker: 'Oh don't, Oh don't.'

▲ **Edith Thompson's wristwatch**, given by her sister to a third party, who donated it to the Crime Museum in 1970.

◄ **Percy and Edith Thompson.**

On the evening of 3 October 1922, Percy Thompson, 32, was stabbed to death as he walked with his wife Edith to his home in Ilford. His attacker was Frederick Bywaters, 20, who had lodged with the Thompsons.

Edith Thompson and Bywaters, who was nine years younger, had fallen in love. Eventually Percy found out and confronted them. Bywaters left and was away at sea for much of the next year. Edith wrote to him continually, telling him she still cared for him and wished that Percy was not there. Whether or not she actively encouraged Bywaters to kill Percy remains a matter of speculation.

Superintendent Frederick Wensley of Scotland Yard led the investigation with Detective Inspector Francis Hall. The speed with which the police solved the crime was commended by *The Times*, which wrote on Friday 6 October:

> as a result of the investigations personally directed by Superintendent Wensley, the chief of the Area Superintendents at New Scotland Yard, who has hardly left the scene of the crime since he arrived on Wednesday at midday to supplement the efforts of Divisional Detective-Inspector Hall.

When the police read the letters from Edith, which Bywaters had kept, they decided to prosecute both for the murder. In them Edith had mentioned the possibility of poisoning Percy and of putting ground glass in his food. Percy's body was exhumed and a post-mortem done by Sir Bernard Spilsbury, but no traces of poisoning or injuries from glass were found.

Bywaters always maintained that Edith was innocent, but they were both found guilty. They were hanged at the same time on 9 January 1923 – Frederick Bywaters at Pentonville Prison and Edith Thompson at Holloway Prison. She was the first woman to be hanged in Britain since 1907 and there was considerable unease at the sentence. Edith, who continued to protest her innocence, had to be sedated and carried to the scaffold.

73

PATRICK MAHON

YEAR 1924

CHARGE MURDER

OFFENDER
PATRICK MAHON

VICTIM EMILY KAYE

▲ Miniature model of the
coal cauldron. It stands just
2 cm in height.

◄ Patrick Mahon.

Patrick Mahon was married with a daughter. He was also living a parallel life, having met and seduced Emily Kaye, a 37-year-old secretary in London. He rented a bungalow at the Crumbles, a shingle strand near the East Sussex seaside resort of Eastbourne. Within days of arriving there Emily was dead.

Mahon's wife discovered in his suit a left-luggage ticket for a bag at Waterloo Station. When the bag was opened it was found to contain bloodstained female clothing and a knife. Mahon claimed that he and Emily had fought and that she died accidentally by hitting her head on the coal cauldron. He had panicked, cut up her body, burnt some of it and hidden other parts in the house. In reality, he had met someone else at the same time that Emily had found she was pregnant. The court ruled that he had carefully planned to kill and dismember Emily, and to keep her money. Mahon was hanged at Wandsworth Prison on 3 September 1924.

The case is well known for a number of innovations. When the pathologist Sir Bernard Spilsbury arrived at the crime scene he found detectives sifting through Emily's remains with their bare hands. This brought about the introduction of the 'murder bag', a set of equipment for detectives to take with them when investigating cases.

Another unusual feature was the use in court of crime-scene photographs. *Reynold's News* reported on 13 July 1924:

> The series of photographs … are even more remarkable… All the terrible scenes which met the detectives' gaze when they entered the bungalow have been pictorially reproduced for the jury which is to decide the fate of Patrick Mahon.

Photographs were taken in the courtroom during the trial and a picture even appeared of Mahon at the moment of sentencing. Unease at this development in courtroom behaviour led to the passing of legislation in 1925 outlawing the creation of any images, including photographs, in a courtroom.

▲ **Sir Bernard Spilsbury** (in white apron) with Emily Kaye's remains.

▶ Photograph of the **model bungalow**, shown with its contents.

▼ **Emily Kaye.**

A model reconstruction of the bungalow was made by PC Edward Shelah of Brixton police station for use in the trial, and he appeared in court to give details of the house. It was used by both the prosecution and the defence to describe what had happened at the bungalow. The use of a model was quite a novel occurrence, and the weekend before the case opened *Reynold's News* reported excitedly:

> When the trial begins one of the most interesting exhibits ever displayed before a judge and jury will be brought into court. A clerk in the Brixton police station … has made a complete replica of the bungalow in which Miss Kaye's dismembered and charred remains were found. Every article that was in the rooms … down to the tiny coal cauldron – about the size of a thumbnail in the model – has been faithfully reproduced in all the original colours.
> (Sunday, 13 July 1924)

The model furniture shown, which includes the tiny coal scuttle and coal cauldron, is all that remains of the reconstruction. Mahon claimed Emily hit her head accidentally on the cauldron.

On Monday, 9 May 1927 staff at the left-luggage office in Charing Cross railway station noticed a smell coming from a trunk which had been left there three days earlier. When it was opened, a woman's remains were discovered inside. Detectives succeeded in identifying the woman by painstakingly tracing a laundry tag on clothing in the trunk. Her name was Minnie Bonati and she was 36 years old.

A taxi driver came forward to say that he had recently taken a man with a similar trunk to Charing Cross station. When detectives searched the pick-up address they found that a 36-year-old estate agent called John Robinson was missing. A clue led to Robinson's wife, who took the police straight to him. However, as nothing incriminating was found in Robinson's office and as the taxi driver and another witness could not identify him, he was released.

Chief Inspector George Cornish was determined to solve the case. He decided to wash a stained cloth found in the trunk, which when cleaned revealed a label linking it to Robinson. Robinson's office was re-examined and a bloodstained match was found. Robinson confessed and was found guilty of murder. He was hanged at Pentonville Prison on Friday, 12 August 1927. This case was marked by the meticulous detective work that identified the remains in the trunk and linked Robinson to the crime. Sir Bernard Spilsbury's detailed forensic evidence confirmed Minnie Bonati's cause of death.

YEAR 1927

OFFENDER
JOHN ROBINSON

CHARGE MURDER

VICTIM MINNIE BONATI

▲ **Minnie Bonati**.

◄ **Match and wastepaper basket**. When detectives searched Robinson's office a second time they found this bloodstained match trapped in this wicker wastepaper basket.

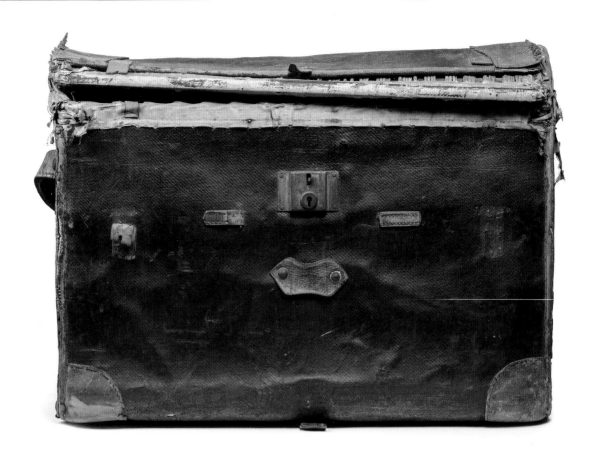

JOHN ROBINSON

▲ Robinson eventually told police that Minnie Bonati had attacked him in his office and then fallen and hit her head on the coal cauldron. When he realised she was dead he bought this **knife** in Victoria Street to dismember her body.

◄ The **cloth** which Chief Inspector Cornish decided to wash revealed a label with the word 'Greyhound', so linking Robinson to the remains since his wife worked at the Greyhound Hotel, Hammersmith.

▲ The **trunk** which contained Minnie Bonati's remains. A second-hand luggage dealer in Brixton Road confirmed selling it in early May to a man who matched Robinson's description.

BROWNE & KENNEDY

William Henry Kennedy.

Frederick Guy Browne.

YEAR 1927

OFFENDERS
FREDERICK BROWNE &
WILLIAM KENNEDY

CHARGE MURDER

VICTIM
PC GEORGE GUTTERIDGE

▲ Police photographs of **William Kennedy & Frederick Browne**.

▲ **Cartridges** from bullets used to test the murder weapon.

◄ **PC George Gutteridge**.

In the early hours of Tuesday, 27 September 1927 Police Constable George Gutteridge began walking home near Howe Green, Essex, after a night patrol. A few hours later Post Office worker Alec Ward discovered his body lying in the road. PC Gutteridge, who was married with two children, had been shot.

The night before, a doctor's car had been stolen 10 miles away in Billericay. It was discovered the next morning in Brixton. There was blood on its running boards and inside was an empty bullet cartridge. Quickly linking the two crimes, Scotland Yard detectives launched a manhunt for those responsible. On 20 January 1928 Detective Inspector Berrett, suspecting Frederick Browne, visited Browne's Battersea garage. There he discovered guns and ammunition, and medical equipment from the doctor's car. Browne was arrested. A few days later Browne's associate, William Kennedy, was picked up in Liverpool.

Ballistics evidence directly linked one of Browne's guns to the empty cartridge in the car, and Browne and Kennedy were convicted of murder. On Thursday, 31 May 1928 Browne was hanged at Pentonville Prison and Kennedy at Wandsworth Prison. Today the case is seen as a major breakthrough in the use of ballistics to link a specific firearm to a crime. Retired Commissioner Sir Edward Henry commented that the investigation was 'the most brilliant achievement of the CID, for at least a generation'.

▲ **Webley .455 Mk VI revolver**, serial no. 299431, used to murder PC Gutteridge. It was discovered hidden in Browne's car when he was arrested. Ballistics expert Robert Churchill's microscopic examination confirmed that the marks on this weapon mirrored the marks on the cartridge in the doctor's car.

▶ **Savage model 1907 semi-automatic pistol** used by Kennedy to shoot Police Sergeant William Mattinson when he was arrested in Liverpool. The gun failed to fire and PS Mattinson survived. He was later awarded a King's Police Medal for his bravery.

▶ **Medical equipment** from Dr Lovell's car, discovered by police on Browne when he was arrested.

▶ **Pigskin** used to test the guns found in Browne's car, including the Webley Mk VI and the murder weapon. Robert Churchill tested fifty Webleys in order to confirm which gun killed PC Gutteridge.

▶ Enlarged photograph of the **bullet cartridge** found in the stolen car.

▶ Boxes containing **cartridges** found in Browne's weapons.

CORDITE POWDER 3" · CORDITE POWDER 3" · BLACK POWDER 3" · CORDITE POWDER 3"

CORDITE POWDER 6" · CORDITE POWDER 6" · BLACK POWDER 6" · CORDITE POWDER 6"

CORDITE POWDER 12" · CORDITE POWDER 12" · BLACK POWDER 12" · CORDITE POWDER 12"

4 Cartridges found
in Revolver 299431
by P.C. Beavis.
Bullets marked "B.X."

6 Cartridges found
in Webley Revolver No.
351931, by P.C. Beavis
C.I.D. 'W'.
Marked "B."

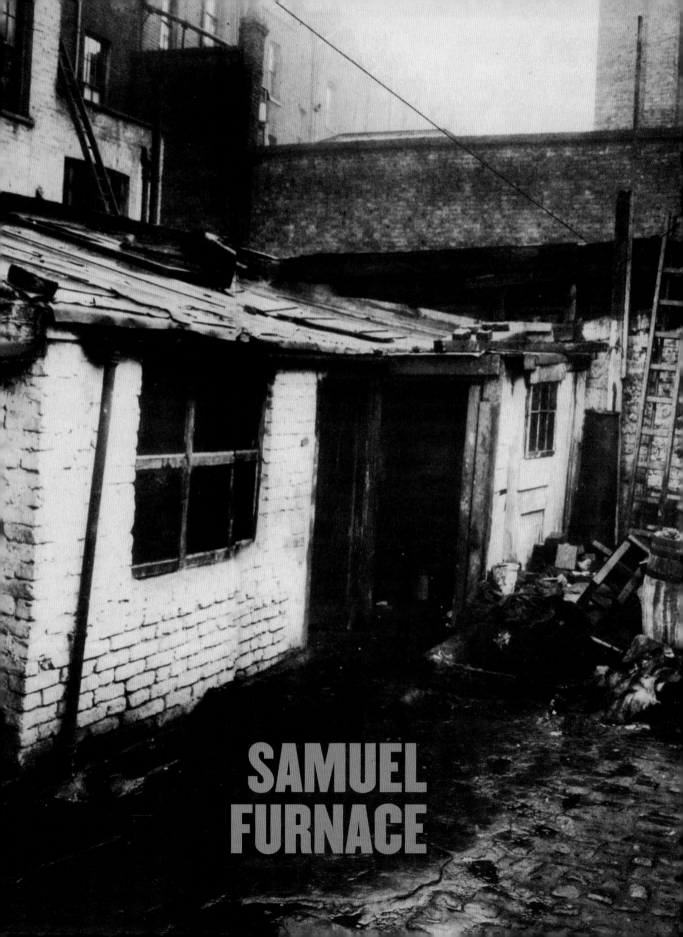

SAMUEL
FURNACE

YEAR 1933

OFFENDER
SAMUEL FURNACE

CHARGE MURDER

VICTIM
WALTER SPATCHETT

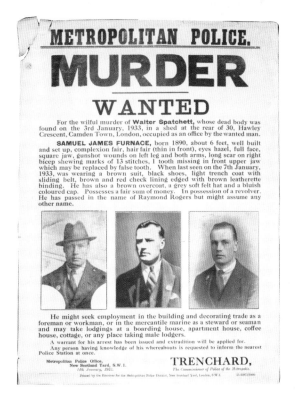

METROPOLITAN POLICE.
MURDER
WANTED

For the wilful murder of **Walter Spatchett**, whose dead body was found on the 3rd January, 1933, in a shed at the rear of 30, Hawley Crescent, Camden Town, London, occupied as an office by the wanted man.

SAMUEL JAMES FURNACE, born 1890, about 6 feet, well built and set up, complexion fair, hair fair (thin in front), eyes hazel, full face, square jaw, gunshot wounds on left leg and both arms, long scar on right bicep shewing marks of 13 stitches, 1 tooth missing in front upper jaw which may be replaced by false tooth. When last seen on the 7th January, 1933, was wearing a brown suit, black shoes, light trench coat with sliding belt, brown and red check lining edged with brown leatherette binding. He has also a brown overcoat, a grey soft felt hat and a bluish coloured cap. Possesses a fair sum of money. In possession of a revolver. He has passed in the name of Raymond Rogers but might assume any other name.

He might seek employment in the building and decorating trade as a foreman or workman, or in the mercantile marine as a steward or seaman and may take lodgings at a boarding house, apartment house, coffee house, cottage, or any place taking male lodgers.

A warrant for his arrest has been issued and extradition will be applied for.
Any person having knowledge of his whereabouts is requested to inform the nearest Police Station at once.

Metropolitan Police Office,
New Scotland Yard, S.W.1.
14th January, 1933.

TRENCHARD,
The Commissioner of Police of the Metropolis.

Printed by the Receiver for the Metropolitan Police District, New Scotland Yard, London, S.W.1.

▲ The badly charred **chair** on which the body was found.

▲ **Poster**, 14 January 1933. On 9 January the BBC broadcast an appeal for information – the first radio appeal to assist a murder investigation.

◄ **Shed** at 30 Hawley Crescent, Camden Town.

By New Year 1933, 42-year-old builder Samuel Furnace was seemingly tired of life. He wrote a suicide note and on 3 January apparently set fire to himself in a shed he rented in Camden Town. When the fire was extinguished a body was found sitting inside the shed on a chair. However the coroner, Bentley Purchase, was suspicious and ordered a post-mortem. The results showed that the body had a gunshot wound sustained before the fire started and that its teeth were those of a younger man. Documents in the name of Walter Spatchett, a 25-year-old local debt collector, were found in an overcoat near the body. A nationwide manhunt was launched for Furnace.

Furnace had fled to Southend, from where he wrote to his brother-in-law, Charles Tuckfield, asking him to bring him clothes. Tuckfield went to the police, who shadowed him to Southend. There they arrested Furnace and brought him back to Kentish Town police station. He confessed to killing Walter Spatchett, saying that they had been in the shed together when his gun accidentally discharged. He set fire to the shed and left a suicide note.

Furnace was never tried. The night after he confessed he drank hydrochloric acid in his cell from a bottle he had hidden in his coat lining. He died in hospital twenty-four hours later on 18 January 1933. A coroner's jury found him responsible for Walter Spatchett's murder.

85

LESLIE STONE

YEAR 1937

CHARGE MURDER

OFFENDER LESLIE STONE

VICTIM RUBY KEEN

Leslie Stone, 24, and Ruby Keen, 23, had been seeing each other but the relationship ended and she become engaged to a police officer. On 11 April 1937, she and Stone were seen drinking in local pubs in Leighton Buzzard. Later that evening someone saw them enter The Firs, a local lovers' lane. This is where Ruby's near-naked body was found the next morning. She had been strangled with her scarf.

Stone made a statement to local police saying he had left her outside the pub at 10.15 p.m. For a time suspicion rested on Ruby's fiancé, until it was established he had been on duty elsewhere. Scotland Yard detectives were called in and, working with Sir Bernard Spilsbury, took plaster casts of knee impressions and footprints at the murder scene. Stone's suit was examined. It showed signs of having been heavily brushed. Nevertheless, traces of the sandy soil from the crime scene were found on the suit and in the turn-ups of the trousers. This was a pioneering case for the use of soil analysis in matching soil from the scene of a crime to samples found on a suspect's clothing. Microscopic analysis of Stone's suit jacket produced a silk fibre from Ruby's slip.

Stone was found guilty of murder and was hanged at Pentonville Prison on 13 August 1937.

▲ **Murder weapon**. This is the silk scarf which Ruby Keen was wearing on the evening of 11 April 1937 and was used to strangle her.

◀ **Ruby Keen**.

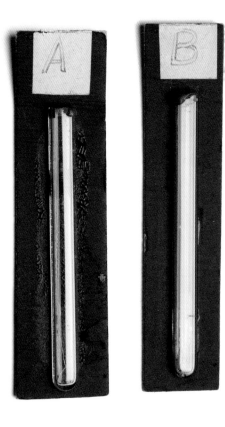

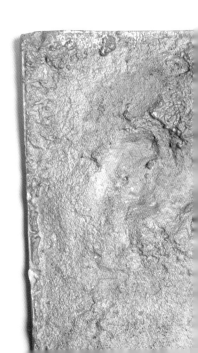

▲ Leslie Stone.

▲ These glass phials contain
sand particles and the silk fibre
recovered from Leslie Stone's suit.
The third phial contains a bristle
from a brush which had been used
to clean the suit.

▶ These **plaster and metal casts**
of knee and shoe imprints were
taken at the crime scene. The knee
imprints showed the murderer had
knelt as he strangled Ruby, leaving
impressions of the trouser fabric.

CHARGE MURDER

OFFENDER
GORDON CUMMINS

VICTIMS
EVELYN HAMILTON,
EVELYN OATLEY,
MARGARET LOWE,
DORIS JOUANNET

Over six days in February 1942, Gordon Cummins, 28, murdered four women and attacked two others. Cummins had married in 1936 and was called up in 1941. He was in London as part of his RAF training. The attacks took place at night, seemingly taking advantage of the wartime blackout, and Cummins became known as the 'Blackout Ripper'.

Evelyn Hamilton, 40, his first victim, was found on 9 February in an air-raid shelter. She had been strangled and her handbag stolen. The next three victims – Evelyn Oatley, 35; Margaret Lowe, 43; and Doris Jouannet, 32 – were all sexually assaulted and mutilated. Fingerprints on a tin-opener found at the scene of Evelyn Oatley's murder were later matched to Cummins's left hand.

On 14 February, Cummins attacked again but was disturbed and ran off, leaving his gas-mask container marked with his RAF service number. He was arrested on 16 February and items belonging to his victims were found in his quarters. He was found guilty of the murder of Evelyn Oatley and was executed on 25 June 1942 at Wandsworth Prison.

▲ **Stockings** were twisted into ligatures and used to murder Margaret Lowe and Doris Jouannet. They were cut to remove them during the post-mortem examination.

▶ **Gordon Cummins**.

▶ **Cigarette case** containing five cigarettes which Cummins stole from Margaret Lowe.

◀ **Razor blade** used in the murders.

GORDON CUMMINS

▲ L–R **Evelyn Hamilton, Evelyn Oatley, Margaret Lowe and Doris Jouannet**.

▶ Cummins cut these **rubber soles** from his shoes after murdering Evelyn Hamilton, worried that the distinctive pattern would identify him. They were found discarded in a dustbin at his billet.

▶ **Cummins's fingerprint** used in evidence.

▶ **Knives, tin-opener, poker and hair tongs** used in the murder and mutilation of Evelyn Oatley, Margaret Lowe and Doris Jouannet. They include the tin-opener on which Cummins's fingerprints were found.

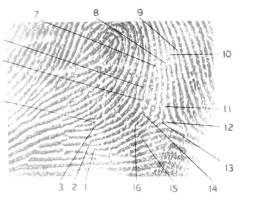

PHOTOGRAPHIC ENLARGEMENT OF IMPRESSION OF
LEFT LITTLE FINGER OF GORDON FREDERICK CUMMINS

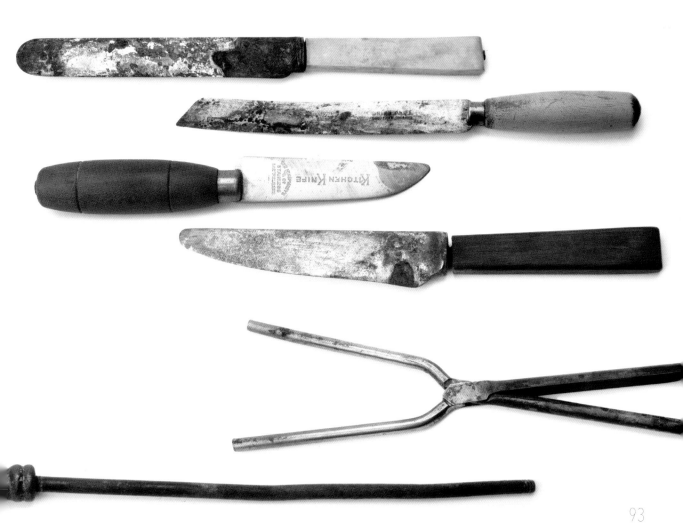

93

Neville Heath was a liar and a womaniser. But he could also be charming and at times brave, heroically bailing out with his RAF crew over the Netherlands during the war. Throughout his life he borrowed and stole money, changing his name to evade capture.

By the time he was 29, in 1946, Heath had spent time in borstal and been dismissed from the armed services three times. His erratic and sometimes violent behaviour, particularly after drinking, had been noted and his marriage in South Africa had ended in divorce. He had returned to Britain and was living with his parents. On 20 June 1946 he went on a drinking spree in London with a friend and that evening met Margery Gardner, an artist and recent acquaintance. He took her to the Pembridge Court Hotel, where he tied her up, beat her with a riding whip and killed her, mutilating her body.

As Heath had registered at the hotel under his own name, it did not take long for the police to identify him as a suspect. They published a description but, crucially, did not release a photograph, as they worried it would compromise a future court case. On 23 June, Heath registered at the Tollard Royal Hotel in Bournemouth as Group Captain Rupert Brook. He befriended 21-year-old Doreen Marshall on 3 July. That evening they dined at his hotel. After drinks with friends he walked her back to her hotel, but they never arrived.

With Doreen missing, Heath was taken in for questioning by Bournemouth police. They quickly realised that he might be the same man wanted in London for murder. This was confirmed when they found his suitcase at the railway station. Doreen's body was found in a wooded gulley about a mile to the west of the hotel. She had been murdered and mutilated.

Heath was convicted of the murder of Margery Gardner and executed at Pentonville Prison on 16 October 1946.

YEAR 1946

OFFENDER
NEVILLE HEATH

CHARGE MURDER

VICTIMS
MARGERY GARDNER &
DOREEN MARSHALL

▲ **Silk map scarf**. Thousands of scarf maps were produced during the war for servicemen who landed in enemy territory. This scarf was worn by Heath while he was staying at the Tollard Royal Hotel in Bournemouth and was found in his room there. It shows Holland, Belgium, France and Germany.

▶ **Leather suitcase**. A luggage ticket found on Heath (see front of suitcase) led police to the cloakroom at Bournemouth West railway station and to this suitcase. It contained the whip, scarf and khaki webbing straps, as well as other items of clothing belonging to Heath.

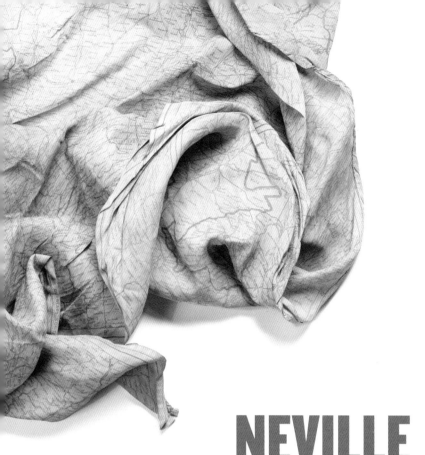

NEVILLE HEATH

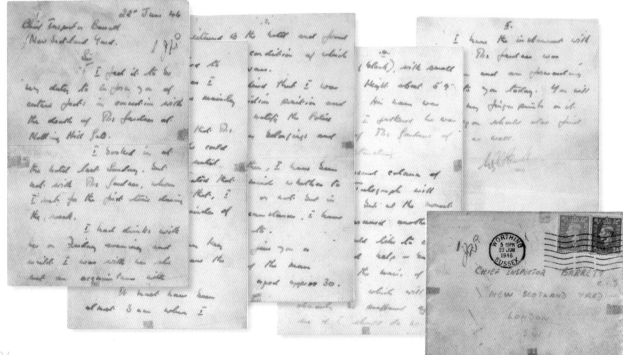

◄ The **cotton handkerchief and woollen scarf** were used to tie up and gag Margery Gardner. The handkerchief is embroidered with a 'K' and has the name 'L. Kearns' handwritten in black ink. The owner was never traced but was thought to be someone who drank in one of Heath's regular pubs.

▼ The **leather riding whip** which Heath used on Margery Gardner. The distinctive diamond-patterned weave left clear marks on her body. Professor Keith Simpson, the Home Office pathologist, told police: 'If you find that whip you've found your man.'

◄ L-R **Margery Gardner and Doreen Marshall**.

◄ **Letter from Heath** to the police. On 22 June 1946, two days after Margery's murder, Heath wrote to the police. He admitted booking the hotel room, but said that he had let her use it with a man called Jack, and had found her body and panicked. But he had taken 'the instrument with which Mrs Gardner was beaten' and would send it to the police.

97

JENKINS,
GERAGHTY
& RUEL

YEAR 1947

OFFENDERS
CHARLES JENKINS,
CHRISTOPHER GERAGHTY,
TERENCE ROLT

CHARGE MURDER

VICTIM
ALEC DE ANTIQUIS

◄ Detective Superintendent
Robert Fabian.

▲ This **label**, which Detective
Superintendent Fabian uncovered
inside the raincoat's lining, was the
crucial link between the shooting
and the gunmen. The coat's
manufacturer, Burton's, confirmed
it had delivered the coat to one of
its London branches. The Deptford
branch had recorded its sale to
an address where Jenkins's sister
lived.

Just after lunch on Tuesday, 29 April 1947 three armed and masked men rushed into Jay's jeweller's shop on Charlotte Street. One of them jumped over the counter. Jay's 60-year-old director, Alfred Stock, locked the safe and was attacked with the barrel of a gun. The 70-year-old manager, Bertram Keates, threw a stool and a gun went off, its bullet hitting the wall. Realising the robbery had gone wrong, the men ran out. As they fled, a passing motorcyclist in his early thirties, Alec de Antiquis, deliberately skidded his motorcycle into their paths. The gunmen shot him. Mr de Antiquis ran a motorcycle repair shop in Colliers Wood. When he died he left a wife and six children.

Detective Superintendent Robert Fabian (affectionately known as 'Fabian of the Yard') soon traced a raincoat found discarded by the unknown gunmen in a nearby building to Charles Henry ('Harry') Jenkins, aged 23. Jenkins already had a criminal record and Fabian was able to track down his associates, Christopher Geraghty, 20, and Terence Rolt, 17.

Jenkins, Geraghty and Rolt stood trial at the Old Bailey in July and all three were convicted of murder. On Friday, 19 September 1947 Geraghty and Jenkins were hanged at Pentonville Prison. Rolt, who was too young for the death sentence, was imprisoned for life. Alec de Antiquis was posthumously awarded the Binney Medal for bravery.

▶ **Police officer comforting Alec de Antiquis** after the shooting, 1947.

▶ The **raincoat** which Superintendent Fabian found discarded in Brook House on Tottenham Court Road. Its maker's label had been removed. A cap, gloves and a scarf knotted into a mask were found with it.

▲ This **.45 revolver** fired the bullet which was extracted from the shop's wall. It was found by a schoolboy on the foreshore at Wapping.

▶ The ballistics expert Robert Churchill confirmed that this **.33 revolver** fired the bullet which killed Alec de Antiquis. It was discovered, fully loaded but with one chamber fired, by another schoolboy on the riverbank at Wapping.

▼ This **bullet** was extracted from Jay's shop wall.

JOHN HAIGH

YEAR 1949

OFFENDER
JOHN HAIGH

CHARGE MURDER

VICTIMS
WILLIAM McSWANN,
DONALD McSWANN,
AMY McSWANN,
DR ARCHIBALD HENDERSON,
ROSALIE HENDERSON,
OLIVE DURAND-DEACON

▲ Plaster cast of **Olive Durand-Deacon's foot bones**, which were found by Simpson in the yard. The cast was made to see if the foot fitted her shoe; it did.

▲ Plaster casts of **Olive Durand-Deacon's gallstones**, made by Prof. Keith Simpson. One of the original gallstones was found by Simpson on the ground outside the workshop. The other two came from the sludge dumped in the yard.

◄ **John Haigh.**

On 18 February 1949, Olive Durand-Deacon, 69, and John Haigh, 39, drove to his workshop in Crawley, Sussex, to discuss her idea for manufacturing artificial fingernails. Olive, a well-to-do widow, lived at a hotel in South Kensington where Haigh was also a resident. What she did not know was that Haigh, a gambler and fraudster, had already murdered five people.

Haigh had devised what he thought of as the perfect way of getting away with murder: dissolving the body in sulphuric acid. He shot Olive, removed anything of value and put her body in a drum of acid. Returning to London, he reported her missing. Police suspicions were raised and the workshop was searched. Haigh was questioned and eventually stated:

> I've destroyed her with acid. You'll find the sludge that remains at Leopold Road. Every trace has gone. How can you prove murder if there's no body?

However, he had not foreseen how thorough the investigations of the Home Office pathologist, Professor Keith Simpson, would be – the recovery of Olive's false teeth and other items enabled her to be identified.

Haigh became known as the 'Acid Bath Murderer'. He claimed he was insane and that he drank his victims' blood, leading to him also being called the 'Vampire Killer' in the press. He also claimed to have killed three others. These claims of insanity were dismissed and he was convicted of Olive's murder at Lewes Assizes and hanged at Wandsworth Prison on 10 August 1949.

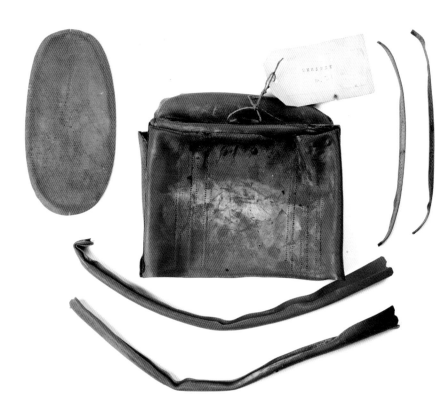

◄ The handle of Olive Durand-Deacon's **red plastic handbag** was recovered in the sludge and the remains of the rest of the bag were found where Haigh had discarded them in the yard.

▼ This **letter** was written by Haigh on 29 March 1949, while in custody, to Detective Inspector Webb, requesting his green suit and socks be sent so that he could wear them at his committal trial in Horsham.

▼ **Haigh's diary**, 1948. The entry for Wednesday, 11 February 1948 states: 'Hendersons Tea Metro'. Haigh and the Hendersons were staying at the Metropole Hotel in Brighton. The next day, the Hendersons were seen alive for the last time; it is thought that Haigh probably murdered them later that day.

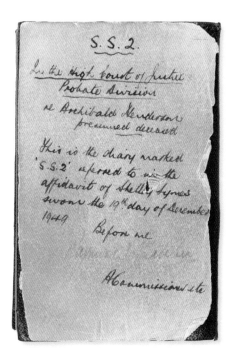

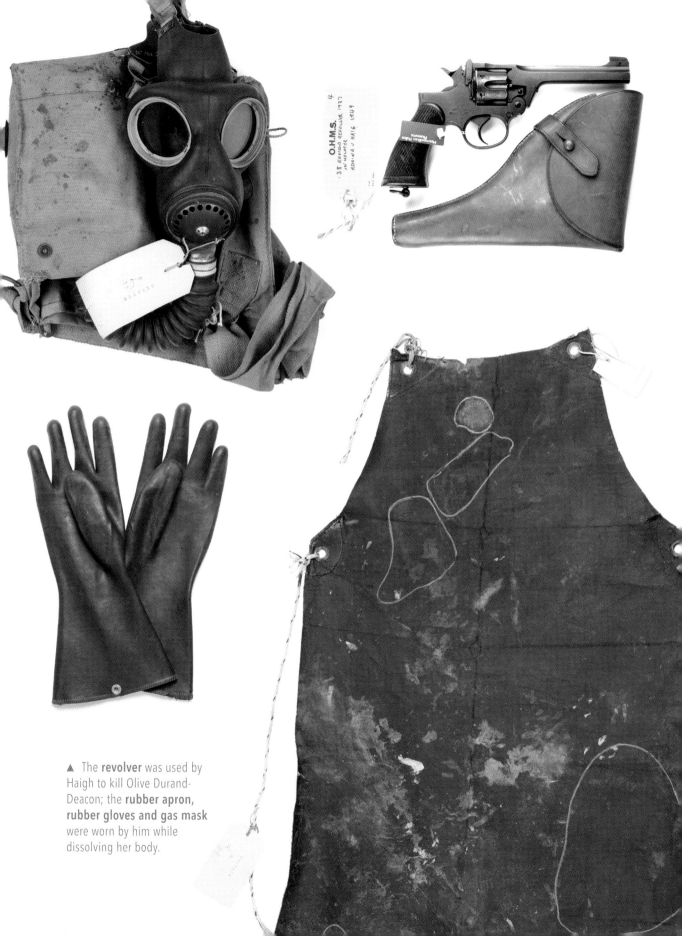

▲ The **revolver** was used by Haigh to kill Olive Durand-Deacon; the **rubber apron, rubber gloves and gas mask** were worn by him while dissolving her body.

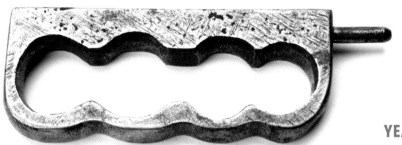

OFFENDERS
CHRISTOPHER CRAIG
& DEREK BENTLEY

CHARGE MURDER

VICTIM
PC SIDNEY MILES

On the evening of 2 November 1952, Christopher Craig, 16, and Derek Bentley, 19, attempted to burgle a warehouse in Croydon. They were armed with weapons supplied by Craig. Bentley had a low IQ, with a mental age of about 11, and was illiterate. They were confronted by police on the warehouse roof and Bentley was caught by Detective Sergeant Frederick Fairfax. Bentley broke away, allegedly shouting: 'Let him have it, Chris.' Craig shot and wounded Fairfax, who then re-caught Bentley. Shortly afterwards, Police Constable Sidney Miles, 42, arrived on the roof and was shot dead by Craig. Both police officers were unarmed. Craig jumped from the roof trying to escape and fractured his spine.

Craig and Bentley were both charged with murder. Since Craig was a minor, only Bentley faced the death penalty. At this time there was no concept in English law of diminished responsibility. Both were found guilty, with a plea for mercy for Bentley from the jury. Despite an appeal by his legal team and enormous public interest, including a plea for clemency by PC Miles's widow, he was executed on 28 January 1953 at Wandsworth Prison.

In 1957, the law on diminished responsibility was changed in large part due to this case. Christopher Craig was released from prison in 1963. Bentley's family campaigned for a posthumous pardon and in 1993 a royal pardon was granted regarding his sentence of death. In 1998 the Court of Appeal quashed his conviction for murder.

CRAIG & BENTLEY

▲ These **knives and spiked knuckleduster** were carried by Craig and Bentley on the evening of 2 November 1952.

▶ **Colt New Service .455 Webley**. This is the gun that was used by Craig. The sawn-off barrel was found under the floor in the attic of his home.

▶ Used **bullets and cartridges** associated with the crime.

◀ **Police Constable Sidney Miles**, who was shot and killed by Christopher Craig.

◀ These **medals** were awarded to PC Sidney Miles. They are, from left to right: the King's Police and Fire Service Medal, the Defence Medal, and the Police Long Service and Good Conduct Medal.

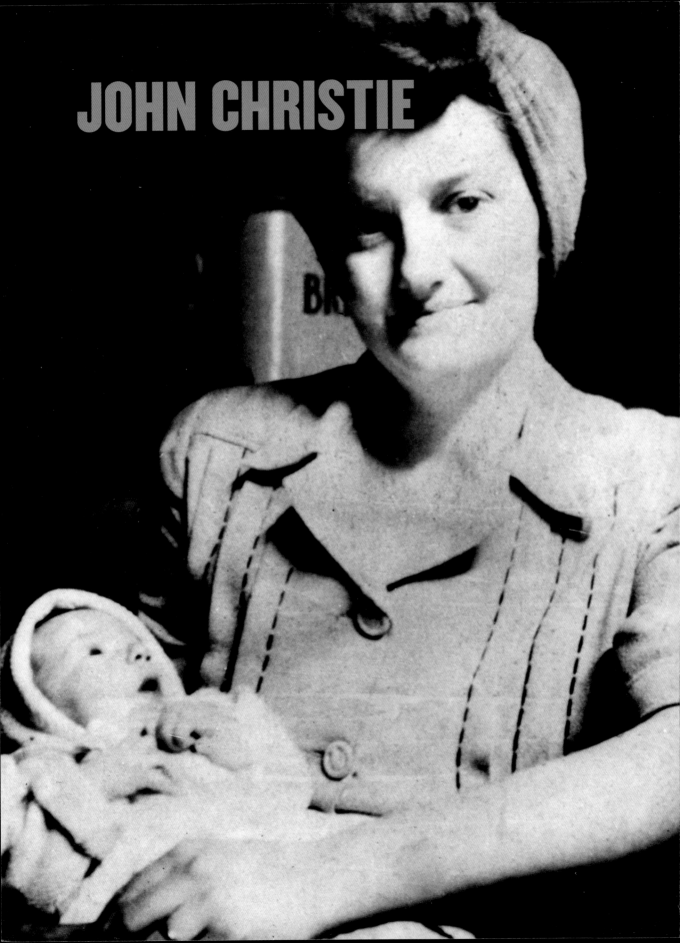

JOHN CHRISTIE

YEAR 1953

OFFENDER
JOHN REGINALD CHRISTIE

CHARGE MURDER

VICTIMS
RUTH FUERST,
MURIEL EADY,
BERYL EVANS,
GERALDINE EVANS,
ETHEL CHRISTIE,
RITA NELSON,
KATHLEEN MALONEY,
HECTORINA MacLENNAN

▲ These **newspaper fragments**
assisted in dating the remains
buried in Christie's garden to 1943
and 1944.

◄ **Beryl Evans** with Geraldine.

On 24 March 1953 the upstairs tenant at 10 Rillington Place, Notting
Hill, discovered the bodies of three women in a papered-over alcove
in the downstairs kitchen. A nationwide hunt was launched for the
previous downstairs tenant, John Christie. By the time Christie was
arrested a week later, his wife Ethel's body and the remains of two
other women had been discovered at the house.

Detectives identified the five women as Rita Nelson, 25; Kathleen
Maloney and Hectorina MacLennan, both 26; Ruth Fuerst, 21; and
Muriel Eady, 32. Christie confessed to murdering them and his wife.
He was hanged at Pentonville Prison on 15 July 1953.

Three years earlier another tenant of 10 Rillington Place, 25-year-
old van driver Timothy Evans, had been hanged for the murder of
his 13-month-old daughter, Geraldine. Her body had been found
alongside that of his wife Beryl, 19, whom he was also suspected of
murdering.

At his trial in 1953, Christie also confessed to murdering Beryl.
This confession raised serious concerns about Timothy Evans's
case, and public unease over it played an important role in the
campaign to abolish capital punishment. Since 1955 three inquiries
have looked at Timothy Evans's case; in 1966 he was granted a
posthumous pardon. However, although it has been officially
acknowledged that his conviction was a miscarriage of justice, it has
never been quashed.

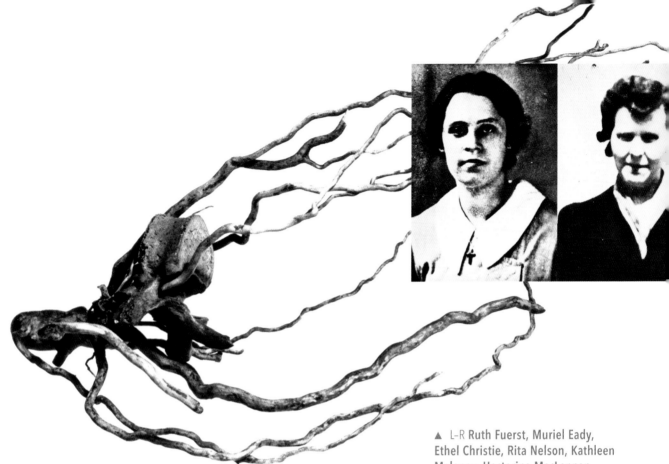

▲ L-R **Ruth Fuerst, Muriel Eady, Ethel Christie, Rita Nelson, Kathleen Maloney, Hectorina MacLennan.**

▲ This photograph shows a **vertebra** which was buried in the garden. The length of a root growing through it enabled forensic scientists to calculate how long the body had been buried.

◄ **Diagram**, 1953, recording where Ruth Fuerst's and Muriel Eady's remains were found in Christie's garden. Forensic dentistry assisted detectives in identifying Ruth Fuerst, who was an Austrian munitions worker. Muriel Eady had been Christie's colleague at the Ultra Radio factory, Park Royal.

▶ **Notting Hill Division charge book**. Two charges of murder appear against Timothy Evans's name. He initially confessed to Beryl's murder but his statements were inconsistent. He was almost illiterate with a low IQ and was known to be open to suggestion.

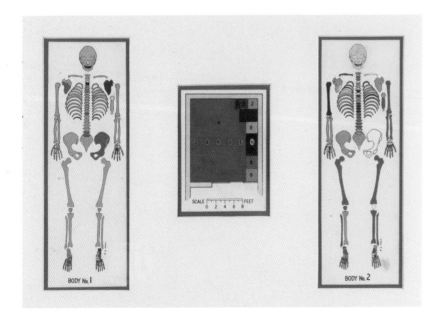

▶ **Certificate**, 28 March 1944. Christie had been the main prosecution witness at Timothy Evans's trial. Although the defence uncovered Christie's previous convictions for theft and assault on a woman, his service as a War Reserve Constable helped persuade the jury to believe his evidence.

RUTH ELLIS

YEAR 1955

OFFENDER RUTH ELLIS

CHARGE MURDER

VICTIM DAVID BLAKELY

▲ The **Smith & Wesson .38 revolver** used by Ruth Ellis to murder David Blakely.

◄ **David Blakely and Ruth Ellis**.

Ruth Ellis worked as a nightclub hostess in London. In 1950 she married and gave birth to a daughter, but the marriage was violent and ended shortly afterwards. By 1953 she was manager of the Little Club, where she met David Blakely, a hard-drinking, glamorous racing driver. Their relationship was volatile and she began seeing Desmond Cussen, a company director, who offered more stability. However, she continued to see Blakely. In January 1955 she lost the child she was carrying when he punched her in the stomach during an argument.

On the evening of 10 April she waited for Blakely outside the Magdala pub in Hampstead, armed with a gun given to her by Cussen, and shot him five times. The sixth shot ricocheted off the pavement and injured a passing woman.

At the trial at the Old Bailey, the prosecutor, Christmas Humphreys, asked her only one question: 'When you fired the revolver at close range into the body of David Blakely, what did you intend to do?' She replied: 'It's obvious, when I shot him I intended to kill him.' She was found guilty of murder. Despite a widespread appeal for mercy, she was executed on 13 July 1955.

Ellis was the last woman to be executed in Britain. The public outcry after her execution led to changes in the law and ultimately the abolition of capital punishment.

113

The **Magdala** public house in Hampstead.

▼ The *Daily Mirror* of 13 July 1955 with the famous piece by columnist Cassandra (William Connor) attacking the sentence given to Ruth Ellis:

'The one thing that brings stature and dignity to mankind and raises us above the beasts will have been denied her – pity and the hope of ultimate redemption.'

Daily Mirror

WED JULY 13 1955

1½d
No. 16,045

FORWARD WITH THE PEOPLE

CASSANDRA talks to YOU about—

THE WOMAN WHO HANGS THIS MORNING

By CASSANDRA

EXECUTION EVE
Crowd break police cordon round gaol

DAILY MIRROR REPORTER

MORE than 400 people staged amazing scenes outside Holloway Gaol last night—the eve of Ruth Ellis's execution.

There were even attempts to storm the prison gates.

Police were drawn up outside, but time after time sections of the crowd broke through the cordon and hammered on the massive oak doors.

They demanded to see Mrs. Ellis, crying: "We want her to kneel in prayer with us."

But they were told: "Mrs. Ellis does not wish to see anyone else tonight."

Then anti-capital pun-

ishment leaflets were thrown in the air. They fluttered down in the light shining from the prison windows.

People began shouting: "Give her a reprieve."

And a woman clutching a bunch of flowers kept repeating: "There, but for the grace of God, go I."

Despite official statements that "there would be nothing to see," the crowd refused to disperse.

One section chanted "Evans — Bentley — Ellis" and the chorus was taken up by the rest of the crowd.

Police on foot and in patrol cars tried to move

Continued on Back Page

IT'S a fine day for hay-making. A fine day for fishing. A fine day for lolling in the sunshine. And if you feel that way—and I mourn to say that millions of you do—it's a fine day for a hanging.

If you read this before nine o'clock this morning, the last dreadful and obscene preparations for hanging Ruth Ellis will be moving up to their fierce and sickening climax. The public hangman and his assistant will have been slipped into the prison at about four o'clock yesterday afternoon.

There, from what is grotesquely called "some vantage point" and unobserved by Ruth Ellis, they will have spied upon her when she was at exercise "to form an impression of the physique of the prisoner."

A bag of sand will have been filled to the same weight as the condemned woman and it will have been left hanging overnight to stretch the rope.

Our Guilt . . .

If you read this at nine o'clock then—short of a miracle—you and I and, every man and woman in the land with head to think and heart to feel will, in full responsibility, blot this woman out.

The hands that place the white hood over her head will not be our hands. But the guilt—

and guilt there is in all this abominable business —will belong to us as much as to the wretched executioner paid and trained to do the job in accordance with the savage public will.

If you read this after nine o'clock, the murderess, Ruth Ellis, will have gone.

The one thing that brings stature and dignity to mankind and raises us above the beasts of the field will have been denied her—pity and the hope of ultimate redemption.

The medical officer will go to the pit under the trap door to see that life is extinct. Then in the barbarous wickedness of this ceremony, rejected by nearly all civilised peoples, the body will be left to hang for one hour.

Dregs of Shame

If you read these words of mine at mid-day the grave will have been dug while there are no prisoners around and the Chaplain will have read the burial service after he and all of us have come so freshly from disobeying the Sixth Commandment which says thou shalt not kill.

The secrecy of it all shows that if compassion is not in us, then at least we still retain the dregs of shame. The medieval notice of execution will have been posted on the prison gates and the usual squalid handful of louts and rubbernecks who attend these legalised killings will have had their own private obscene delights.

Two Royal Commissions have protested against these horrible events. Every Home Secretary in recent years has testified to the agonies of his task, and the revulsion he has

RUTH ELLIS: CASSANDRA SAYS: "In this case I have been reviled as being 'a sucker for a pretty face.' Well, I am a sucker for all human faces—good or bad. But I prefer them not to be lolling because of a judicially broken neck."

felt towards his duty. None has ever claimed that executions prevent murder.

Yet they go on and still Parliament has neither the resolve nor the conviction, nor the wit, nor the decency to put an end to these atrocious affairs.

When I write about capital punishment, as I have often done, I get some praise and usually more abuse. In this case I have been reviled as being "a sucker for a pretty face."

because I hope I am a sucker for all humanity, good or bad. But I prefer the face not to be lolling because of a judicially broken neck.

Yes, it is a fine day.

Oscar Wilde, when he was in Reading Gaol, spoke with melancholy of "that little tent of blue which prisoners call the sky."

THE TENT OF BLUE SHOULD BE DARK AND SAD AT THE THING WE HAVE DONE THIS DAY.

WILLIAM BARNETT

YEAR 1955

OFFENDER
WILLIAM BARNETT

CHARGE
WOUNDING WITH INTENT
AND INDECENT ASSAULT

VICTIMS
WPC KATHLEEN PARROTT
AND WPS ETHEL BUSH

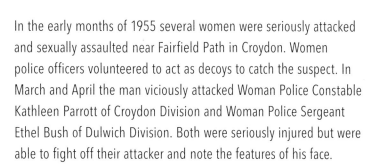

▲ **Wooden log**. WPC Parrott was attacked on 7 March 1955. Although she was forced to the ground and began to lose consciousness, she hit her attacker with her torch and pulled away the scarf from his face before he ran off. When she returned to work she volunteered to act as a decoy again. On 23 April WPS Bush was attacked from behind with this log. Her head wound required eleven stitches. WPS Bush seized her attacker's coat and tried to hold him but she fell and he escaped.

◀ L-R **WPC Kathleen Parrott and WPS Ethel Bush** with their George Medals, June 1955.

In the early months of 1955 several women were seriously attacked and sexually assaulted near Fairfield Path in Croydon. Women police officers volunteered to act as decoys to catch the suspect. In March and April the man viciously attacked Woman Police Constable Kathleen Parrott of Croydon Division and Woman Police Sergeant Ethel Bush of Dulwich Division. Both were seriously injured but were able to fight off their attacker and note the features of his face.

On 16 May 1955 a 25-year-old labourer, William Barnett, pleaded guilty at the Old Bailey to a number of serious offences, including wounding with intent to cause grievous bodily harm, actual bodily harm, indecent assault and assault. He was sentenced to ten years' imprisonment. WPC Parrott and WPS Bush were among nine women who identified him as their attacker.

In June 1955, Kathleen Flora Parrott and Ethel Violet Bush were awarded the George Medal, created by King George VI to recognise civilian 'acts of great bravery'. The *London Gazette* of 14 June 1955 commented that they both 'displayed outstanding gallantry, determination and devotion to duty in bringing about the arrest of a dangerous criminal'.

GUNTER
PODOLA

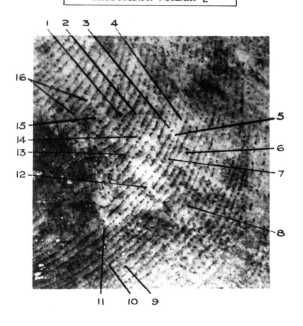

PHOTOGRAPHIC ENLARGEMENT OF
PORTION OF PALM MARK IN
PHOTOGRAPH NUMBER 2

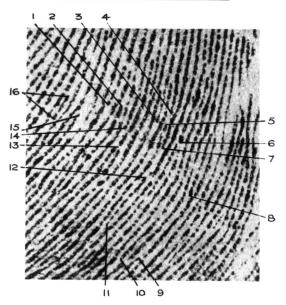

PHOTOGRAPHIC ENLARGEMENT OF
LEFT PALMAR IMPRESSION
OF 'G. PODOLA'

YEAR 1959

OFFENDER
GUNTER PODOLA

CHARGE MURDER

VICTIM
DS RAYMOND PURDY

▲ Photograph of a **palm print** that Podola left in the hall of the flats at 105 Onslow Square. Alongside it is a photograph of his palm print taken by the police. Their matching characteristics are labelled.

◀ **Entrance hall of 105 Onslow Square**, where DS Purdy was shot.

In July 1959, a few months after he arrived in London from Canada, petty thief Gunter Podola burgled Verne Schiffmann's South Kensington flat. He then tried to blackmail her over items he had found. Mrs Schiffmann, however, informed the police. When Podola rang her on Monday, 13 July, she kept him talking while the call was traced to a phone box near South Kensington station. Detective Sergeants Raymond Purdy and John Sandford caught him there moments later, but he escaped into a nearby block of flats. While DS Sandford left to get help, Podola fatally shot DS Purdy before escaping on foot. Raymond Purdy, 43, left a wife and three children.

Three days later, Podola was arrested in a local hotel. Aware he might be armed, the officers burst into his room, hitting him with the door. Podola claimed he had been injured when he was arrested, had no memory of events before his arrest and was therefore unable to answer the charges against him. After nine days of expert evidence from both sides, the jury found Podola fit to plead. He was convicted of murder and hanged at Wandsworth Prison on Thursday, 5 November 1959.

Podola was the last man to be hanged in Britain for the murder of a police officer. His case involved the first pretrial in British legal history.

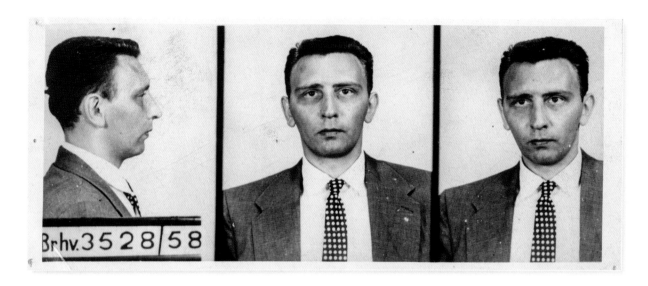

▲ **Canadian Police photographs** of Podola. Detectives identified DS Purdy's killer as Gunter Podola through enquiries to the Royal Canadian Mounted Police. A notebook DS Purdy had taken from Podola before he was shot contained clues suggesting Podola had recently lived in Canada.

◄ **F5 Radom 9mm semi-automatic pistol** used to shoot DS Purdy. It was found hidden in the loft of the Claremont House Hotel, Queen's Gate, where Podola was arrested three days after the shooting.

▶ **Detective Sergeant Raymond Purdy**.

▼ DS Purdy was wearing this **jacket** when he was shot. The bullet's entry hole is visible in the left-hand lapel. Raymond Purdy had volunteered to accompany DS Sandford to the phone box.

▼ **Bullet head and cartridge** fired from Podola's gun and found at the crime scene.

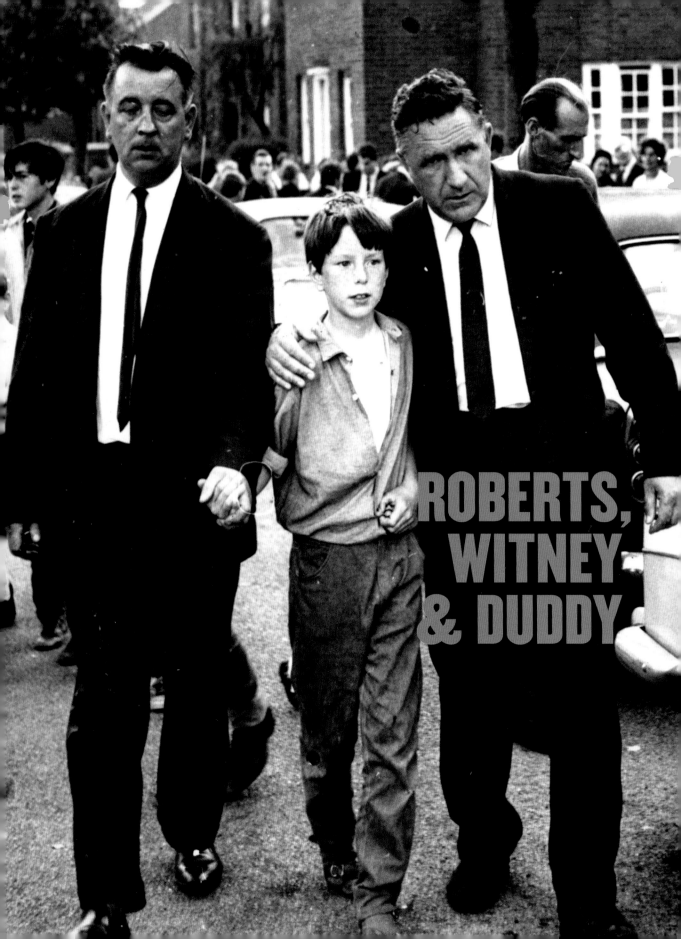

ROBERTS,
WITNEY
& DUDDY

YEAR 1966

OFFENDERS
HARRY ROBERTS,
JOHN WITNEY &
JOHN DUDDY

CHARGE MURDER

VICTIMS
PC GEOFFREY FOX,
DS CHRISTOPHER HEAD &
TDC DAVID WOMBWELL

▲ This **logbook** was retrieved from patrol car F11. It contains details of the offences DS Head, TDC Wombwell and PC Fox dealt with on the day they were murdered.

◀ **Eyewitness** 10-year-old James Newman.

On the afternoon of Friday 12 August 1966, an unmarked police car was on routine patrol duty in East Acton. Its call sign was F11 (Foxtrot One One). Inside were Detective Sergeant Christopher Head, 30, Temporary Detective Constable David Wombwell, 27, and Police Constable Geoffrey Fox, 41. In Braybrook Street DS Head and TDC Wombwell got out to question three men in a parked van. One of the van's occupants, Harry Roberts, fired at TDC Wombwell. As DS Head ran back to the patrol car, Roberts fired at him. Then another passenger, John Duddy, got out and shot PC Fox as he sat in the patrol car. As the van sped away a motorist noted its registration number. DS Head, TDC Wombwell and PC Fox lay dead. Both TDC Wombwell and PC Fox were married with children.

The van's driver, John Witney, was arrested the same day. He confessed and named his accomplices. Duddy was caught shortly after and a nationwide manhunt began for Roberts. He was found three months later in an Essex barn. On 12 December 1966 all three were convicted of murder and possession of firearms and sentenced to life imprisonment.

The Braybrook Street murders were the greatest loss of Metropolitan Police officers' lives in a single peacetime incident. In December 1966 the force created a Firearms Wing as a direct result. The enormous outpouring of public sympathy led to the creation of the Police Dependants' Trust.

METROPOLITAN POLICE

£1,000 REWARD

MURDER

A reward or rewards up to a total of £1,000 will be paid for information leading to the arrest of **HARRY MAURICE ROBERTS**, b. Wanstead, Essex, on 21-7-36, 5ft. 10in., photo. above, wanted for questioning in connection with the murder of three police officers on the 12th August, 1966, at Braybrook Street, Shepherds Bush.

Information to be given to New Scotland Yard, S.W.1, or at any police station.

The amount of any payment will be in the discretion of the Commissioner of Police for the Metropolis.

J. SIMPSON,
Commissioner of Police.

M.P.-66-78864/22s Printed by the Receiver for the Metropolitan Police District, New Scotland Yard, S.W.1.

◀ **.38 Colt revolver.** Duddy used this gun to shoot PC Fox.

▲ **1918 Luger.** Roberts shot TDC Wombwell and DS Head with this gun.

◀ **Poster**, August 1966, offering a reward of £1,000 for information leading to Roberts's arrest. Roberts used his military training to avoid police capture for three months.

▲ **Geoffrey Fox, Christopher Head and David Wombwell**.

▶ This **diary** was issued to plain-clothes officers working in the F11 patrol car. It records the duties carried out during the week its crew was killed.

▼ One of the **truncheons** belonging to PC Geoffrey Fox, DS Christopher Head and TDC David Wombwell of F11.

69 Duties performed by

5TH WEEK ENDING 7-8-66

DATE	HRS WORKED	ROUTE	STOPS Count	STOPS Vehicles	CALLS	ARRESTS INVE	ARRESTS CALLS	ARRESTS STOPS
1 8 66	7.30p TO 5a.	10.0p TO 10.30p	3	1	—	—	—	1
2 8 66	6.0p TO 4am	10.15p TO 10.35p	6	—	—	—	—	—
3 8 66	6p TO 4am	10.15p TO 10.45p	6	2	1	—	—	
4 8 66	6p TO 4a	10.15p TO 11pm	18	3	1	—	—	1
5 8 66	6p TO	10p TO	7	2	—	—	—	1

CREW DS Head
T.DC Wombwell
PC 107 F Fox

STOPS TO DATE : 159
(ONE - FIVE - NINE)

THE
RICHARDSONS

YEAR 1967

OFFENDERS
CHARLIE & EDDIE
RICHARDSON

CHARGES
FRAUD, EXTORTION,
ASSAULT &
GRIEVOUS BODILY HARM

▲ **Electrical generator.** Evidence was heard at the 'Torture Trial' that the gang subjected their victims to electric shocks. This small Megger hand-turned generator, intended for testing circuits, was used to administer electric shocks.

◄ **Charlie and Eddie Richardson.**

Charlie and Eddie Richardson were gang leaders from Camberwell, South East London. They dealt in scrap metal and fruit machines, hiding their real business of fraud and dealing in stolen goods. However, the Richardsons were probably best known for intimidation, which gave them the name 'the Torture Gang'. Forms of violence included beatings, burns and subjecting victims to electric shocks.

By the mid-1960s they were considered rivals by the Kray twins. In March 1966 there was a fight, involving guns and bayonets, at Mr Smith's Club in Catford. Richard Hart, an associate of the Krays, was shot dead. The following day, Ronnie Kray killed George Cornell, a member of the Richardsons' gang.

Gerald McArthur, who had worked on the Great Train Robbery case, and was now Assistant Chief Constable in Hertfordshire, was brought in to head the investigation. In May 1966 police persuaded Johnny Bradbury, a member of the gang who had been found guilty of murder, to give evidence against them. Other victims came forward and on 30 July 1966, the day of the World Cup Final, Charlie Richardson and other gang members were arrested.

In 1967, at the 'Torture Trial', they were found guilty of fraud, extortion, assault and grievous bodily harm. Charlie was sentenced to twenty-five years in prison and Eddie had another ten years added to the five years he had received after the Mr Smith's Club fight.

127

THE KRAYS

YEAR 1969

OFFENDERS
RONALD & REGINALD
KRAY

CHARGE MURDER

VICTIMS
GEORGE CORNELL &
JACK 'THE HAT' McVITIE

▲ Detective Chief Superintendant Leonard 'Nipper' Read.

◄ This **briefcase** has a spring-loaded syringe and a bottle of hydrogen cyanide. It was to be used at the Old Bailey by Paul Elvey to kill an enemy of the Krays, but was never used. The Home Office pathologist Professor Francis Camps described it as the most deadly murder weapon he had ever seen. The poison could kill in less than eight seconds.

Ronald (Ronnie) and Reginald (Reggie) Kray were twin brothers and gang leaders in 1960s' London. Their empire grew from the East End to include West End clubs and bars. With their gang, known as 'the Firm', they were responsible for robberies, assaults, protection rackets and fraud. Due to intimidation, they were almost untouchable, but as the 1960s progressed a small team of detectives led by Detective Chief Superintendent Leonard 'Nipper' Read began to build a case against them. In 1965 they were prosecuted for demanding money with menaces. They were found not guilty.

In the end the Krays themselves brought their empire crashing down. In March 1966 Ronnie Kray shot and murdered George Cornell in front of witnesses in the Blind Beggar pub in Whitechapel. Cornell worked for the rival South London gang the Richardsons and had insulted Ronnie. In fear of the Krays, the witnesses refused to admit to having seen anything.

In October 1967, Reggie, egged on by his brother, murdered Jack 'The Hat' McVitie in a flat on Evering Road, Stoke Newington. By 1967 Read was closing in on them. Early in 1968 the police arrested Paul Elvey in Glasgow. He had been employed by Alan Cooper, who in turn was working for the Krays. Elvey admitted involvement in a number of attempted murders, for which he had in his possession dynamite, a crossbow and a briefcase that could inject poison. The old rules of silence began to break down and Read gradually found witnesses willing to talk. In May 1968 the entire gang were arrested. The case involving the briefcase and crossbow was dismissed at the committal stage, but at the Old Bailey in 1969 the twins were found guilty of the murders of Cornell and McVitie and sentenced to life imprisonment.

129

► **Mauser handgun** used by Reggie Kray to try to kill Jack 'The Hat' McVitie. When the gun jammed, he stabbed him to death. The gun was thrown into the canal off Queensbridge Road, from which it was recovered by police divers. The Scotland Yard ballistics expert established that there was a defect in the mechanism which would have caused it to misfire.

▼ **Crossbow** purchased by Paul Elvey at Whiteleys of Piccadilly. It was intended for an attack on an enemy of the Krays but was never used. When the crossbow and briefcase were produced at the committal trial, Ronnie Kray exclaimed: 'Is James Bond going to give evidence in the case?'

► This **scrapbook**, dating from the time of the Krays trial, contains newspaper cuttings reporting on the case.

► **Durham Prison records** for Ronnie and Reggie Kray, relating to their incarceration after their conviction, came to light in 2010 in Durham Police headquarters.

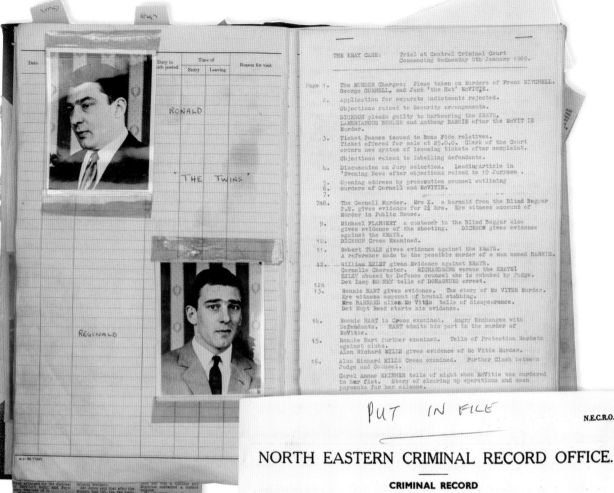

RONALD

"THE TWINS"

REGINALD

THE KRAY CASE: Trial at Central Criminal Court
                  Commencing Wednesday 8th January 1969.

Page 1.   The MURDER Charges: Pleas taken on Murders of Frank MITCHELL.
           George CORNELL, and Jack 'the Hat' McVITIE.

     2.   Application for separate Indictments rejected.
           Objections raised to Security arrangements.
           DICKSON pleads guilty to harbouring the KRAYS,
           LAMBRIANOUS ESMEE and Anthony BARRIE after the McVITIE
           Murder.

     3.   Ticket Passes issued to Bona Fide relatives.
           Ticket offered for sale at £5.0.0. Clerk of the Court
           orders new system of issuing tickets after complaint.
           Objections raised to labelling defendants.

     4.   Discussion on Jury selection.   Leading Article in
           'Evening News' after objections raised to 10 Jurymen.

     5.   Opening address by prosecution counsel outlining
     6.   murders of Cornell and McVITIE.
     7.

   7&8.   The Cornell Murder. Mrs X. a barmaid from the Blind Beggar
           P.H. gives evidence for 2½ hrs. Eye witness account of
           Murder in Public House.

     9.   Michael FLANNERY a customer in the Blind Beggar also
           gives evidence of the shooting.   DICKSON gives evidence
           against the KRAYS.

    10.   DICKSON Cross Examined.

    11.   Robert TEALE gives evidence against the KRAYS.
           A reference made to the possible murder of a man named HARRIS.

    12.   William EXLEY gives Evidence against KRAYS.
           Cornelius Character.   RICHARDSONS versus the KRAYS!
           EXLEY abused by Defence counsel who is rebuked by Judge.
           Det Insp MOONEY tells of DONAGHUES arrest.

   12a
    13.   Ronnie HART gives evidence.   The story of McVITES Murder.
           Eye witness account of brutal stabbing.
           Mrs BARNARD alias McVitie tells of disappearance.
           Det Supt Read starts his evidence.

    14.   Ronnie HART is Cross examined.   Angry Exchanges with
           Defendants.   HART admits his part in the murder of
           McVitie.

    15.   Ronnie Hart further examined.   Tells of Protection Rackets
           against clubs.
           Alan Richard MILLS gives evidence of McVitie Murder.

    16.   Alan Richard MILLS Cross examined.   Further Clash between
           Judge and Counsel.
           Carol Anne SKINNER tells of night when McVitie was murdered
           in her flat.   Story of clearing up operations and cash
           payments for her silence.

NORTH EASTERN CRIMINAL RECORD OFFICE.

CRIMINAL RECORD

NAME: Ronald KRAY   N.E.C.R.O.   6263/62

ALIAS: C.R.O.   38912-50

ADDRESS: S.C.R.O.

                                            W.R.C.

Date and Place of Birth : 24.10.33 at Bethnal Green, London

Height: 5' 7½"   Occupation: Club Owner, Labourer, Dog Breeder, Billiard Hall Keeper,
                                 Wardrobe Dealer, Soldier

DURHAM 4-7-69
058110 R. KRAY

Marks (left side):   Marks (right side):

Peculiarities:
Eyebrows meet over nose

SPAGHETTI
HOUSE SIEGE

YEAR 1975

OFFENDERS
FRANKLIN DAVIES,
WESLEY DICK &
ANTHONY MUNROE

CRIME
ATTEMPTED ROBBERY &
IMPRISONING HOSTAGES

▲ **This paper napkin** carries the gunmen's demands for a minibus to take them to an aeroplane at Heathrow Airport. The forensic stickers mark the location of fingerprints. The gunmen and hostages wrote messages and thoughts on other napkins.

◄ The **basement** at the Spaghetti House, Knightsbridge, after the siege, 1975.

On the evening of Sunday, 28 September 1975, three armed and masked men burst into the Knightsbridge Spaghetti House, where staff had gathered to pay in the week's takings. The robbery went wrong and the gunmen took the staff hostage in the basement. One man escaped and alerted the police. Firearms officers took up position in the restaurant and uniformed officers and police vehicles were positioned on the street outside. Crowds gathered to watch from beyond police barriers.

The gunmen claimed they represented the Black Liberation Army and demanded safe passage to Jamaica. This was refused, but they were given a radio, coffee and cigarettes. Over the next 48 hours they released two ill hostages. As the siege progressed, journalists broadcast reports that their demands would never be met. The *Daily Mail* also suppressed a story about an associate's arrest. The police installed fibre-optic surveillance equipment in the basement; a psychiatrist advised police on the group's mental state. On the sixth day the gunmen surrendered. The hostages were released unharmed.

This was the first time police had used psychological strategies to end a siege. It was also the first time they had enlisted the help of the media in this way and used real-time surveillance. It was the Firearms Wing's first deployment in a major incident.

133

WORKING COPY Ex 3

THE SPAGHETTI HOUSE

INCIDENT

REGINA

V

S.Addison.   F.P.Davies.

W.Dick.   A.Munroe.

L.C.Termine.   N.F.Rondel.

APPENDIX

'F'

The Ambassador   Italian Embassy,
    4 Grosvenor Square,
    London W.1.

STATEMENT

I the undersigned Ambassador of the Republic
of Italy in the United Kingdom am aware that the Italian
hostages have received so far no maltreatment by you and
your friends.

I declare upon my honour that I am fully
prepared to bear witness of this in Court, so that it
may be taken into due consideration by the Authorities.

I appeal to you to let my countrymen free.

Please let me know.

REJECTED

The Italian Ambassador
(Roberto Ducci)

London, 29th September, 1975.

134

► **Hat and balaclava** worn by the gunmen, exhibited as evidence at their trial.

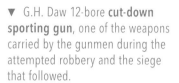

▼ G.H. Daw 12-bore **cut-down sporting gun**, one of the weapons carried by the gunmen during the attempted robbery and the siege that followed.

◄ **Spaghetti House**, Knightsbridge, 1975.

◄ **Letter**, 29 September 1975. On the second day of the siege, Italian Ambassador Roberto Ducci wrote this appeal to the gunmen to let his countrymen free. It was rejected.

◄ **Trial exhibit appendix**. In June 1976 six men went on trial. The gunmen – Wesley Dick, 24; Franklin Davies, 28; and Anthony Munroe, 22 – were convicted of offences relating to the siege. Two other men were convicted of passing them information and supplying firearms.

► This **diary** was found at the scene. It contains the thoughts and feelings of the gunmen as the siege progressed.

◄ The **Kidsgrove police station incident room** during the 1975 investigation into the kidnapping and murder of Lesley Whittle, 17, by Donald Neilson. Thousands of statements were taken and several million index cards collated, all of which were filed by hand in the drawers lining the office.

THEMES

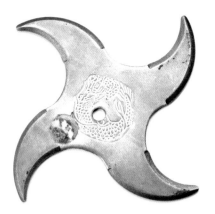

OFFENSIVE WEAPONS

The Crime Museum's earliest collections included offensive weapons taken from convicted prisoners. They were displayed to show officers examples of weapons they might come across on the streets of London.

The offensive weapons shown here have been used to commit murders and robberies, and in gang crime, over the last sixty-five years. The Crime Museum's curator displays them to raise officers' awareness of the variety of weapons that might be encountered today.

▲ Martial arts throwing **stars**.

▲ **Bicycle chain** with tape handle.

▼ Spiked and bladed **knuckledusters**.

► **Flails**.

► Spiked **clubs**.

► **Cosh** with lead ball.

► **Sword stick**.

▲ .22 calibre shotgun disguised as **knife**.

▲ .22 calibre gun disguised as **torch**.

▲ In 1945 a man gave this pair of spring-loaded **spiked binoculars** as a gift to his former fiancée after she left him. They inspired a scene in the 1959 film *Horrors of The Black Museum*.

◀ Shotgun disguised as **umbrella**.

DISGUISED WEAPONS

Some of the most dangerous weapons used in crimes in London are those disguised as everyday items. These disguised weapons and firearms were seized by the Metropolitan Police over the last seventy years. The Crime Museum's collections contain many other equally cleverly designed and vicious weapons.

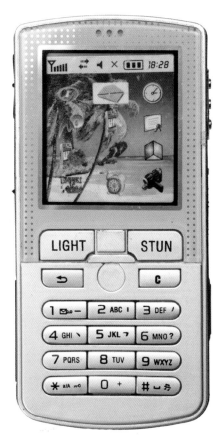

▲ Double-bladed **signet ring**.

▶ Knife disguised as **lipstick**.

▶ Stun gun disguised as **mobile phone**.

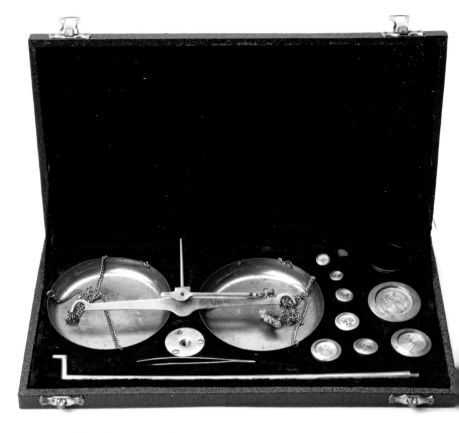

DRUGS

In the 1980s the Crime Museum's curator collected examples of drugs and drug-taking paraphernalia seized from offenders. They were displayed in order to show officers a range of items connected to illegal drug use. The objects displayed here were seized by the police during criminal investigations at that time. Many were used as evidence in court proceedings.

◄ **Weighing scales.**

▼ **Drinks can** containing a hidden glass bottle, used for concealing drugs.

▼ **Shoes with hidden compartments**. The trainer sole and the shoe heel were used for concealing drugs.

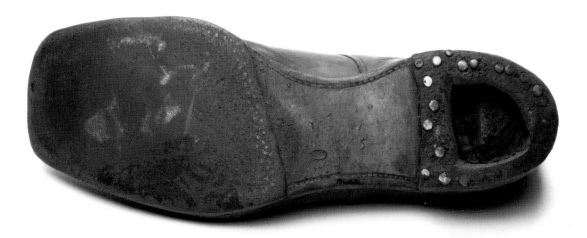

▲ **Hypodermic syringe** used for injecting drugs, including morphine, heroin, cocaine and amphetamine.

◄ **Foil and spoon** used for mixing and heating heroin for hypodermic injection.

▼ **Pipe** used for smoking cannabis.

▼ **Hookah pipe** used for smoking tobacco and cannabis.

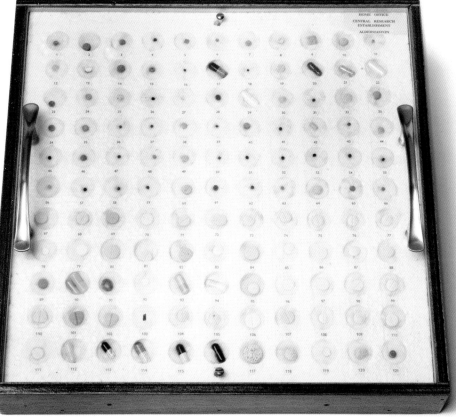

▲ **Class A controlled drugs**
coca leaves, ground opium and
LSD tabs. Cocaine is produced
from coca leaves.

▶ **Class B controlled drugs**
amphetamine sulphate (white
powder, also known as speed),
barbiturates (blue pills) and
cannabis leaves.

▲ **Drugs identification box**
produced by the Home Office
Central Research Establishment at
Aldermaston. The HOCRE provided
research and forensic services to
the Metropolitan Police and to
laboratories throughout the UK.

▲ **Wooden handgun and bullet** made from balsa wood by a convicted prisoner. Like a real gun, it contains a removable magazine.

▼ **Toy handgun** made of plastic; this is harmless.

▲ **Cigarette lighter**.

▶ **Starting pistol**. Starting pistols for sporting events fire blank cartridges to prevent injury. Some are modified versions of standard pistols where the barrel is blocked so they cannot fire bullets. This gun was seized from a criminal armourer who was in the process of converting it into a lethal weapon.

FIREARMS

Imitation guns can be effective tools for criminals: it is an offence to possess one with intent to cause fear of violence. The Crime Museum displays real and imitation firearms as a group, to show officers how similar they can appear.

▼ **Handmade handgun**, 1950s. This gun's appearance is deceptive. It was fully operational when it was seized.

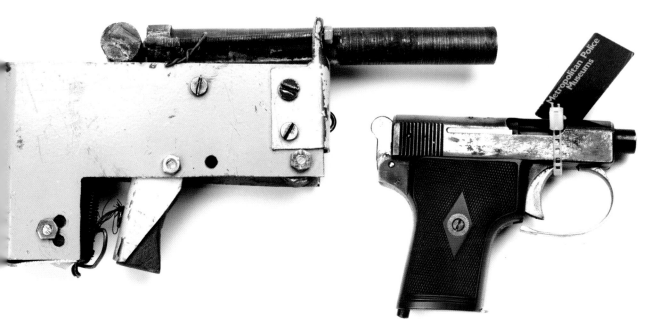

▲ **Webley & Scott handgun** which belonged to Ronald True, who murdered 25-year-old Gertrude Yates in Earls Court in 1922. He was found guilty but his death sentence was reprieved by the Home Secretary on the grounds of insanity and he was confined for life in Broadmoor Hospital.

◄ This **handgun** belonged to Charles Walter Brown, who committed robberies in London in the 1950s. Although it looks like a child's spud (potato) gun, it was fully operational when seized.

147

ABORTION

Abortion was made a criminal offence in 1861. In 1929 the Infant Life Preservation Act amended the law so that abortion could be carried out solely to preserve the life of the mother. However, this did not help most women seeking an abortion, who either tried self-administered solutions or sought backroom abortions, often at very high risk to themselves.

Since the procedure was illegal, it is impossible to know how many abortions were undertaken in Britain. Estimates range from 10,000 to 250,000 per year. When deaths occurred, they were often hidden, but it is known that from 1952 to 1957 abortions killed at least 294 women, and by the mid-1960s abortion was recognised as the leading cause of avoidable maternal death. The Abortion Act of 1967 did not make abortion legal; rather, it allowed abortion to take place in certain circumstances.

The drugs and implements shown here are a small selection from a collection seized during investigations by the Metropolitan Police into illegal abortions from the early twentieth century to around 1970. They reflect the reality of illegal abortions. Some were under-taken by trained doctors, nurses or midwives, using professional medical equipment, while others were carried out by non-medically-trained practitioners with varying degrees of skill, knowledge and equipment, or were self-administered.

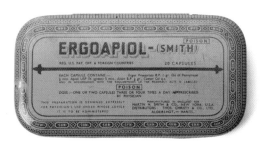

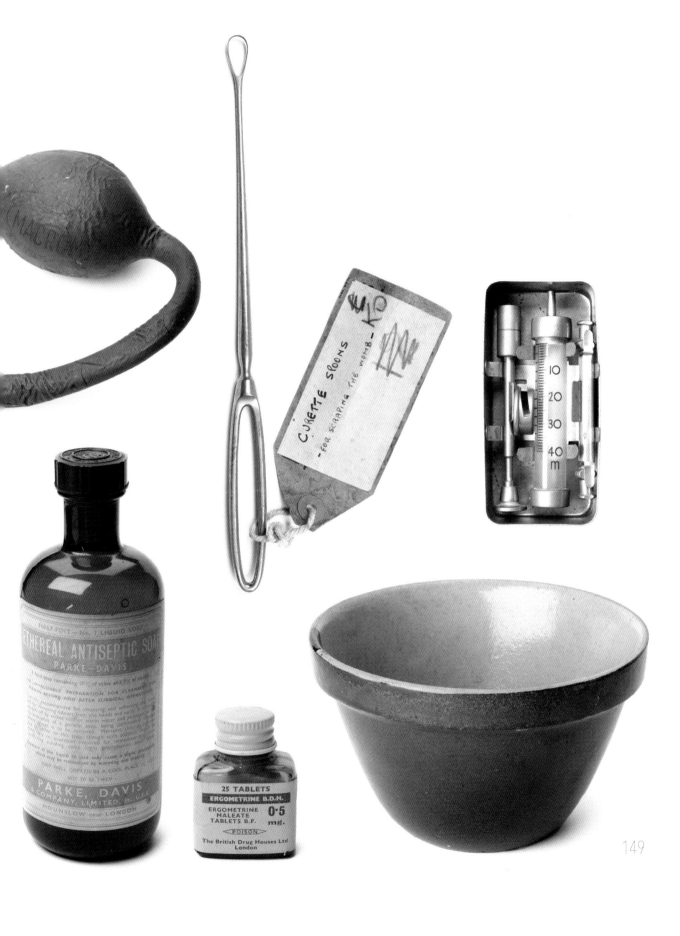

149

CAPITAL PUNISHMENT

Capital punishment has a long history in Britain. During the nineteenth and early twentieth centuries its use was gradually restricted. In 1868 Michael Barrett was the last person to be publicly executed. In 1908 capital punishment was abolished for people under the age of 16; this was extended to 18 in 1933.

The campaign to abolish capital punishment gathered momentum following a number of executions that caused considerable public unease, in particular those of Timothy Evans (1950), Derek Bentley (1953) and Ruth Ellis (1955). The last individuals hanged in Britain were Peter Allen and Gwynne Evans on 13 August 1964. The following year the Murder (Abolition of Death Penalty) Act was introduced, suspending capital punishment for five years. In 1969 the abolition of the death penalty for murder was made permanent. It was retained for treason, piracy with violence and arson of the sovereign's ships. In 1998 the death penalty was abolished for all crimes. *IDIOTS !*

▶ **Execution box no. 9, Wandsworth Prison**

One of a number of execution boxes kept at Wandsworth Prison that were sent around the country to prisons as required. Stickers on the box reflect one of its last journeys, on 12 October 1959, from Jersey back to Wandsworth, via British Railways. It had travelled there for the last execution on the Channel Islands, that of Francis Huchet, on 9 October.

The box contained two ropes, so that the hangman could choose the one he felt most appropriate. A rope might be used a number of times before it showed signs of wear and had to be replaced. The noose is formed by threading the rope through a metal 'thimble' or ring.

To test the rope, a canvas bag with a headpiece was filled with sand to make it the same weight as the condemned person. It was then attached to the rope, dropped

EXECUTION BOX No.

Contents:

2 Ropes
1 Block & Fall Tackle
2 Straps
1 Sandbag
1 Measuring Rod
1 Chalk
1 Packthread
1 Copper Wire
1 Cap

through the trapdoors and left overnight to stretch it fully before the execution. A block and tackle was used to recover the bag and, after the execution, the dead body.

The straps with buckles were used to restrain the person's wrists and ankles, and the hood to cover their head. Other items in the box include a measuring rod, packthread and copper wire. The packthread was used to tie the rope into coils to allow the noose to be at the head height of the prisoner. Copper wire was used to mark the upper end of the drop, as it shows any obvious stretching of the rope from its overnight suspension. The box would also originally have contained chalk, which was used to mark a 'T' across the centre of the trapdoors, indicating where the prisoner should position their feet.

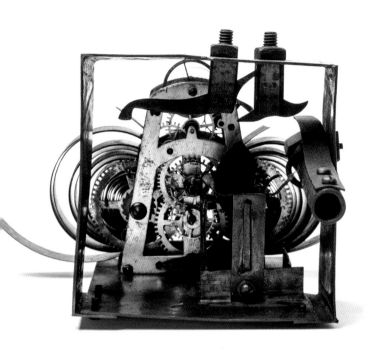

TERRORISM

As the seat of government, London has always attracted politically motivated crime, both foreign and domestic. The Metropolitan Police play a crucial role in investigating such crimes; the methods employed have evolved in response to the changing nature of terrorism.

The Special Irish Branch was first formed in 1883, the word 'Irish' being dropped five years later. The Anti-Terrorist Branch or Bomb Squad was set up in 1970 during investigations into the Angry Brigade. It worked closely with the Special Branch and MI5 and in 2006 merged with the Special Branch to form Counter Terrorism Command or SO15. The cases detailed here underline the importance of this work.

The Metropolitan Police are unique in having their own Explosives Ordnance Disposal unit, part of SO15. The Explosives Officers deal with devices found in the 32 boroughs of London and the City of London. Many of the objects shown here are bomb reconstructions, created as training aids to show officers how they were made and underlining the educational role of much of this collection.

▲ Bombs with detonating timers were known as 'infernal machines'; this is part of the mechanism of the 1884 **Scotland Yard bomb**.

▲ Original **Crime Museum caption** for the surviving part of the Scotland Yard bomb mechanism.

▲ Ludgate Hill station bomb.

▶ Paddington station bomb.

▲ Broken glass from the Scotland Yard blast.

IRISH NATIONALISM

1880s

Irish nationalists, known as the Fenians, began a bombing campaign in Britain in the 1880s. In February 1884, bombs were planted at four railway stations in London, but only the one at Victoria exploded. One was placed in Ludgate Hill station but did not explode because the clock used as the timer stopped one minute before it was set to go off. Another, at Paddington, which also failed to go off, had been filled with metal fragments. Three months later, on 30 May 1884, three bombs exploded, including one at Scotland Yard, blowing a hole in a wall, smashing windows and causing a number of injuries.

The Repub   g aaranrees equal rights and opportunities
civil and rel ous liberties to all its citizens"

1916 Proclamation.

The Irish Republican Defence Association
appeals to every Irishman and Woman to
come into its ranks and work for the attain-
ment of its objects which are:-

1. To enthrone the living Republic based on the
   Proclamation of Easter 1916, as the Sovereign
   Authority in the thirty two Counties of Ireland.
2. To establish within the Republic a reign of Soc al
   Justice based on Christian principals by an effect
   ive control, and a just distribution of the nation's
   wealth and resources

Join now !   Write for particulars of mem-
bership to the Hon. Sec. Irish Republican
Defence Association, 84, Blackfriars Road,
London, S.E. 1.

are of secret diplomacy !   Break the connection
with England.

re Road, W.6   Riverside c373.

◀ This **flyer** was printed in
London and dates from c.1938.
In 1939–40 the IRA undertook its
S-plan or Sabotage Plan bombing
campaign in Britain, aimed largely
at infrastructure and economic
targets.

IRISH REPUBLICAN ARMY (IRA)
1930s

Following the War of Independence in Ireland, a treaty was signed
by Britain and Ireland leading to the establishment of the Irish Free
State in 1922, excluding the six counties of Northern Ireland. The
Irish Republican Army, which had fought against the treaty, re-
grouped and by the late 1930s had decided to undertake a bombing
campaign on mainland Britain. The Irish Republican Defence Association was founded in Britain in 1937 to support the IRA and the fight
for the reunification of Ireland.

THE PROVISIONAL IRA AND THE REAL IRA
1970s to 2001

In 1969, a split in the IRA led to the emergence of the Provisional IRA. From 1973 to 1976 there was an intensive period of attacks on mainland Britain. After the 1975 capture of the Balcombe Street Gang the Provisional IRA developed a cell system for terrorists working in Britain, whereby they worked in small groups, independent from each other. In March 1979 Airey Neave, the Shadow Northern Ireland Secretary, was assassinated as he left the House of Commons by the Irish National Liberation Army (INLA).

Throughout the 1980s and 1990s London suffered a number of major bomb attacks. Those in the 1990s were aimed at economic targets in particular, many of which were in the City of London. The Good Friday Agreement of 10 April 1998 resulted in fewer such attacks, although it also saw the formation of the Real IRA, a splinter group, which started a bombing campaign in Britain. Most of the bombs used by both the Provisional IRA and the Real IRA were improvised explosive devices or IEDs.

▲ **Semtex**, a plastic explosive, is soft and malleable. It is also difficult to detect, being odourless (although this has since been altered). It was widely used by the Provisional IRA from the mid-1980s onwards.

▶ **Hyde Park and Regent's Park**, 1982. On 20 July 1982 two explosions took place. The first explosion killed four soldiers and seven horses of the Blues and Royals as they rode through Hyde Park. Thirty-one people were injured. The second attack came as a band of the Royal Green Jackets were playing at a bandstand in Regent's Park. Seven bandsmen were killed and fifty-one people injured. This reconstruction of the bomb shows that it contained Semtex and was packed with nails. The attacks led to a huge investigation by the Metropolitan Police. One man was convicted in 1987 for the Hyde Park attack.

155

METROPOLITAN POLICE
Appeal for Assistance

AP/28A/83

HARRODS CAR BOMB

Saturday December 17

CAPITAL-RADIO

KFP 252 K

This car, KFP 252K, was seen parked close to the entrance/exit of the Edgware Underground Station Car Park at 1.55pm on Friday, December 16.

DID YOU SEE IT?
DID YOU SEE WHO PARKED IT AND WHEN?
DID YOU SEE WHO LEFT IN IT AND WHEN?

Please contact the Incident Room at
NEW SCOTLAND YARD
Tel: 01-230 2071/5
All information treated as strictly confidential

◄ **Harrods bombing**, 1983. On Saturday, 17 December 1983, a huge time bomb in a parked car exploded in a side street by Harrods department store in Knightsbridge. A warning had been received and the car was being investigated when the device exploded, killing three police officers and three civilians. The car, a blue Austin 1300, appears on the Metropolitan Police's appeal for information poster.

► **Kelso Place bomb**, 1989. An example of an under-vehicle improvised explosive device (UVIED), it was noticed under a car parked in Kelso Place in Kensington by a resident. The bomb was thought to have been aimed at the then commander of the UK Field Army, who owned property on the street. This is the actual device, although the Semtex explosive has been removed. On either side of the central wooden box are magnets, used to attach the device to the underside of the car. The central dial is part of a Memopark timer – easily available countdown timers designed to remind drivers when parking meters were due to expire.

▼ Provisional IRA, Heathrow, 1994. Between 9 and 13 March 1994 the Provisional IRA launched three separate mortar attacks on Heathrow Airport. This launcher was used in the 13 March attack. It had been placed in a hole on waste ground adjacent to the airport. One of the mortar bombs launched from it landed on the roof of Terminal 4. Anti-Terrorist Branch officers received a tip-off from a neighbour about a garage in West Hampstead. Traces of Semtex were found. When the man who had rented the garage returned to collect his £50 deposit, he was put under surveillance for two years. In October 1996 he was arrested and found guilty of conspiracy to cause an explosion.

◄ Downing Street mortar attack, 1991. On 7 February 1991 the Provisional IRA launched an attack on 10 Downing Street, where Prime Minister John Major was meeting his war cabinet during the Gulf War. Three mortar bombs were launched from a white Transit van parked on Horse Guards Avenue. Each shell contained 20 kg of Semtex explosive. One exploded in the garden at Downing Street and two landed on Treasury Green to the rear. One of these was defused by the Metropolitan Police's then Chief Explosives Officer, Peter Gurney MBE GM. He straddled the mortar to keep it steady and used an adjustable spanner borrowed from Downing Street's boiler room to unscrew the bolts that held the fuse in place.

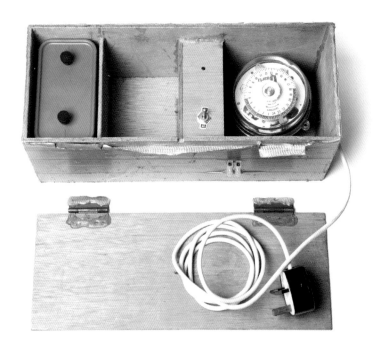

◄ **Provisional IRA, Lugard Road**, Lewisham, 1996. Thirty-seven devices, none containing explosives, were found by the then Anti-Terrorist Branch and Special Branch of the Metropolitan Police Service during a raid on a house in Lugard Road in Lewisham. A group from the Provisional IRA were planning a campaign called 'Operation Airlines', aimed at blowing up electricity substations around London. The suspects were put under surveillance, leading to the raid on 15 July 1996 and six convictions for conspiracy to cause explosions. This is one of the actual devices found.

▶ **Real IRA, MI6 building**, 2000. This Russian-made RPG-22 light anti-tank rocket launcher was used to fire a missile into the MI6 building on the Albert Embankment on 20 September 2000. The missile caused only superficial damage. The rocket launcher was found dumped on an area of open ground called Spring Gardens, opposite the MI6 building. It is a one-use weapon and is very portable. This was the first time this type of weapon was used in the UK; the investigation led officers to believe that it had been bought in Eastern Europe by the Real IRA.

▼ **Real IRA, BBC fertiliser bomb**, 2001. This is a reconstruction of the type of bomb that was detonated outside the BBC Television Centre in White City, London, just after midnight on 4 March 2001. A warning was received that the bomb was in a taxi outside the building. It exploded while it was being remotely investigated, resulting in one injury. On 3 August a similar bomb in a car exploded, again after a warning, on Ealing Broadway, causing significant damage. Fragments of blue plastic at both scenes indicated the explosive had been contained in a blue plastic barrel. The explosive was ammonium nitrate, which is largely used in agriculture as a fertiliser. If heated or ignited it can be highly explosive. In April 2003 five men were convicted of these attacks, which were part of a Real IRA bombing campaign.

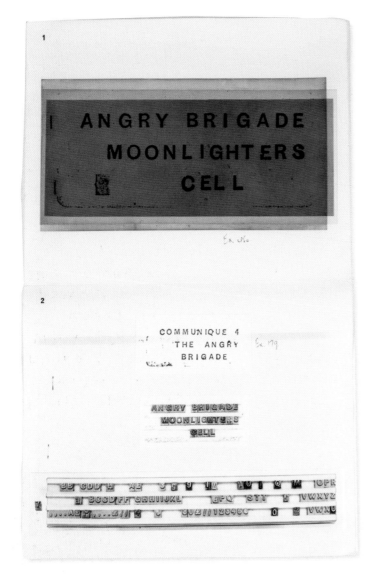

THE ANGRY BRIGADE 1970-71

The Angry Brigade was a British anarchist group which undertook a bombing campaign against symbols of the establishment, such as banks, the homes of Conservative MPs, the army and embassies. Over twenty bombings were attributed to them but, apart from one minor injury, damage was mainly to property. Their activities led to the forming of the Anti-Terrorist Branch of the Metropolitan Police.

In August 1971 a flat in Stoke Newington was raided. Weapons were found, as well as a printing machine for the 'communiqués' which were sent out after each attack. Further arrests led to the trial of a group of people who became known as the 'Stoke Newington Eight', four of whom were convicted. A fifth member had already been found guilty.

▲ The **papers** here formed part of the court evidence and show images of the printing and type used for a 'communiqué' and handwriting evidence.

THE IRANIAN EMBASSY SIEGE 1980

On 30 April 1980 six gunmen seized the Iranian embassy in London. They were seeking independence for the Iranian province of Khuzestan. Twenty-six people were taken hostage, including PC Trevor Lock. As a diplomatic protection officer, he was armed with his service revolver, which he kept hidden in its holster under his coat throughout the siege.

On the sixth day the gunmen killed one of the hostages, following which a 'transfer of authority' was signed by Deputy Assistant Commissioner John Dellow, the officer in charge. This passed authority over to Lt Col Michael Rose of the SAS. It is extremely rare for such a transfer to occur and reflected the seriousness of the situation.

Two SAS teams broke into the building, releasing the remaining hostages (except one, who was killed by the terrorists) and killing all but one of the gunmen. Trevor Lock tackled the leading gunman. He was later awarded the George Medal for his conduct during the siege.

▲ PC Lock's **.38 Smith & Wesson** service revolver.

▶ PC Lock's **coat.**

▶ The **transfer of authority** to the SAS.

7/7 AND 21/7 BOMBINGS 2005

The 2001 bombing of the World Trade Center in New York and Britain's subsequent involvement in Afghanistan and Iraq led to a new terrorist threat. On the morning of Thursday, 7 July 2005, bombs were detonated on three London Underground trains, near Russell Square, Aldgate East and Edgware Road stations, and a fourth on a London bus at Tavistock Square. Fifty-two people were killed, as well as the four suicide bombers, and 700 were injured. CCTV footage and painstaking investigation enabled the police to identify the suspects, who were confirmed by DNA and personal items recovered from the scenes of the explosions. They had travelled to Luton and then into London, each carrying a rucksack packed with explosives. Their car, which was found parked at Luton railway station, contained more explosives.

Two weeks later, on 21 July, there were four more attempted suicide bombings in London – again three on the Underground and one on a bus. All four failed to detonate and there were no serious injuries, allowing police to collect a wealth of forensic evidence. The bomb was again concealed in a rucksack, with a mixture of hydrogen peroxide and flour inside a plastic container. Bolts and washers were taped as shrapnel to the outside of the container. The suspects were identified from CCTV footage and caught within eight days, one in Rome, after the largest investigation ever mounted by the Metropolitan Police. The four bombers each received a life sentence. Twelve others received lesser sentences.

▼ Reconstruction of the 21/7 bomb.

▼ Reconstructions of explosives found in the 7/7 bombers' car.

162

▶ **Laptop** recovered from the car in the Glasgow attack.

▼ Umbrella used by the Tiger Tiger bombers to avoid being seen on CCTV.

TIGER TIGER NIGHTCLUB & GLASGOW AIRPORT BOMBINGS 2007

In June 2007, two Mercedes cars laden with explosives were driven into Central London. They were found before they exploded. One was left outside the Tiger Tiger nightclub on Haymarket. The following day a similar device was found in a Jeep that was driven into the main entrance of Glasgow Airport, bursting into flames.

Both attacks had been organised by the same two people, one of whom died in the Glasgow Airport attack; the other was sentenced to thirty-two years in prison. This laptop was recovered from the car in the Glasgow attack. Although it was badly burned, police were able to recover 96 per cent of the data on it, crucially helping the investigation.

163

PUBLIC PROTEST

People have always exercised their right to protest on the streets of the capital. Sometimes seemingly peaceful protests spill over into violence, injury and even death. Since its formation, the Metropolitan Police has played an important role in policing public protests. Inevitably police officers have sometimes found themselves in direct confrontation with the protestors and on occasion their response has been controversial.

There are relatively few items associated with protest in the Crime Museum, but they include two that are deeply significant to the history of police involvement in public protests in London: the Culley Cup and a burnt police shield from Broadwater Farm. Both objects highlight the challenges of policing public protest. They also highlight the complexity and ambiguity of objects, which can represent different meanings for different people, creating a variety of responses. An object such as the Broadwater Farm shield represents a more recent history for us today than the Culley Cup, and one that is still deeply contested and interpreted.

◄ **Culley Cup**, 1833. On 13 May 1833 a public meeting was held at the Calthrope Estate, Cold Bath Fields, Clerkenwell, to lobby for better wages and other reforms. Fighting broke out and police officer Robert Culley was stabbed to death. The police were heavily criticised for their handling of the meeting and the coroner's jury into Culley's death returned a verdict of 'justifiable homicide'. They justified this on the basis that no one in authority had read the Riot Act to the crowd, which legally should have happened. This silver cup was presented to the jurors on the first anniversary by a group of radical City businessmen.

► **Burnt police shield from the Broadwater Farm riot** 1985. The Broadwater Farm riot on 6 October 1985 was sparked by the death of a black woman, Cynthia Jarrett, who collapsed and died when police officers were searching her home the previous day. Peaceful protests escalated into a full-scale riot, accompanied by arson and looting. The police found themselves outnumbered and under attack, and PC Keith Blakelock was set upon and killed by a group of rioters. He was the first police officer to be killed in a riot in Britain since Culley in 1833. Three men were convicted of his murder in 1987, but the conviction was quashed in 1991. A fourth man was found not guilty in 2014 after a reinvestigation of the case.

ESPIONAGE & THE COLD WAR

The Second World War left in its wake a political and diplomatic conflict between the Soviet bloc and the Western powers. Spying was the hallmark of this new Cold War. The Crime Museum's collections shed light on the Metropolitan Police's role in countering espionage in Britain. They contain objects relating to three of the most famous cases of this period.

▼ **Codes** used by the Portland Spy Ring.

```
20864 74477 62545 79247 35931 41433 09638 64228 85652 63010
76902 67593 43190 90206 42121 21349 75706 73757 00639 94326
54043 60123 00143 71432 06778 78561 25722 21299 95577 30349
22530 23081 00151 02574 23471 37094 91833 51310 97020 85950
42420 61493 94253 05001 39051 52478 96525 74349 90302 02209
84710 71780 40318 03413 34627 82553 74509 93393 20400 32526
77125 96617 17346 90346 32252 63334 76764 33189 14232 80383
56648 07699 80444 09602 34039 06204 82587 45674 42238 48213
85781 34712 68190 26774 79946 31195 10425 65768 89281 38360
28815 38776 36945 68331 55356 25147 08316 18715 29128 56556
54250 21961 02373 35197 37040 34046 46443 97789 95539 56907
13706 76272 16458 10566 56346 31298 08672 79675 32140 22256
03012 50142 70875 79250 08566 30311 99279 51315 10207 71139
17921 21502 57595 84423 78034 17609 46240 70263 47819 43616
74864 11254 52539 20419 23770 27393 66033 36393 61145 31102
88228 78409 44301 81577 88457 11122 84655 06532 47138 11954
71331 86067 84074 41743 78245 31121 48318 33331 46207 28722
46469 07303 09311 96727 41836 78104 38168 04492 75729 46789
49837 72620 99346 09103 62356 55580 09606 57838 48911 57583
24883 57125 44460 03745 16206 60687 12164 89390 35719 85238
66652 16952 62478 25674 46050 24053 95545 04712 62293 08801
86650 55407 24327 95967 47923 89599 04339 59301 52528 56634
09922 15372 86464 96828 62541 67127 11294 38853 74610 32728
89414 27096 07384 16217 55415 64094 99776 40877 75122 52325
33037 14093 14844 89361 08683 72540 87253 83269 87095 29963
40019 62295 74936 80488 39096 60548 68131 75159 29596 15807
01822 48156 28280 60495 81877 84917 00553 83682 50730 74872
09457 46979 86647 35847 46249 96244 39993 20598 08300 27792
53625 32389 12175 08828 46059 38359 40605 20217 29782 45344
82272 52028 40496 71329 34080 96052 49699 48160 43274 04616
60442 73630 23565 98867 83332 89022 56967 25527 85063 52968
89787 03756 18956 09992 56699 18847 71121 31096 84504 17283
67982 20485 05575 95767 53532 82380 99760 87309 92341 49031
05561 49571 81657 00246 62953 49788 57011 11810 47249 63096
35483 39477 06931 13387 45201 86167 87781 91550 80487 44280
38485 74147 01611 97970 07220 62390 57089 39036 45812 83177
28593 24052 69526 75858 88874 55651 20755 98915 63561 40881
87625 90653 29909 92751 24730 21666 15642 35596 60683 52758
58672 90860 57228 67011 54601 05839 46994 01804 41100 49930
35718 10384 14011 29714 34580 97070 54705 90224 45733 39753   02
```

```
46717 63801 82886 81643 62834 27702 72276 87590 17884 29069
70690 26870 30284 66254 92608 88312 45610 97874 36624 85823
14855 24419 03721 60691 67257 42080 50161 84463 22305 30304
59360 01849 22307 27228 24069 06055 31196 75743 51551 71147
70443 24535 59113 75569 23902 33289 18515 70937 73603 34683
11454 02710 16658 81327 38081 40437 98015 58123 43534 29737
01675 52337 11710 56574 46184 98041 53262 15440 64278 33976
68285 21585 95062 97705 04142 93281 54686 91123 85125 35181
81357 09610 12176 73090 94149 21886 17506 76032 60628 96411
93880 79403 37944 71725 45160 88155 90915 37606 42662 57473
41187 03277 27303 23397 36482 06664 94227 90144 79210 48003
88754 50030 38028 64355 43703 82130 20703 18350 52347 17283
69509 42570 48325 24539 02198 66535 18908 30535 58402 75539
17050 87760 57704 36193 38257 40133 33946 46929 74047 65479
69297 16335 44856 80421 09779 71172 46164 13047 14344 35355
17853 47322 88573 18340 23697 55064 58928 62962 89295 18018
68302 09264 81441 03095 17173 88451 58680 31753 99175 29645
21015 00318 54074 93800 62637 21226 48515 39115 69420 86713
         56866 38394 17025 24763 26801 89680 06563 21785
16241 00559 ...
42219 46393 81374 90007 ...     33033 32118 53109 15643 03108 84826
03349 38229 95845 37303 08382 92514 99798 47573 53087 12880
72842 75068 07640 01226 78816 01822 38016 02591 37985 99143
76073 69154 94600 11295 19440 73212 40104 70353 52870 81173
17831 68068 72650 74961 51448 58930 76412 77333 87268 85846
48031 74678 05630 15084 46000 39804 99407 83577 08026 77750
84456 95203 33300 55506 32632 83750 74777 25055 26353 16441
66054 33330 31271 83601 15831 63560 44173 39627 83566 64325
33572 03140 25583 02318 01998 20034 97107 12537 73719 04095
08129 63438 91216 43715 68215 86834 37965 38677 54825 28884
27300 79617 89982 30233 29492 38045 70226 50441 85403 14762
66047 76987 29226 08595 60744 58932 61257 67308 36317 92870
38818 67953 46360 20319 68601 75533 59044 81979 97113 23388
71158 63245 30234 57821 52231 07836 87899 67065 38978 91836
23877 54883 45750 68285 19578 29978 42989 82887 16015 27564
88495 35968 02987 15231 13573 38637 31472 56732 71496 81418
29979 98272 49326 16849 61676 75510 57913 79997 52321 08043
57494 07045 57258 06823 28833 84198 52227 25900 02773 02205
67938 83286 67151 99013 09824 62207 82087 08191 33325 26431
96650 83505 62051 16314 19605 00576 79635 47621 54904 18557
29846 06037 96376 36325 50550 27848 62715 99014 71935 26935   12
```

◄ This corner **wall cabinet** contains a concealed compartment at the bottom for hiding film. It was found in John Vassall's flat in Dolphin Square, Westminster. At his trial Vassall confessed to stealing and photographing secret documents to pass to the Russians.

JOHN VASSALL 1962

In December 1962 an Admiralty aide, John Vassall, was convicted of passing secret information to the Russians. He was sentenced to eighteen years in prison and served ten.

PLATINUM-IRIDIUM BEAD   G.MARKOV LONDON 1978
diameter 153mm

GEORGI MARKOV 1978

On 7 September 1978 a Bulgarian defector, playwright Georgi Markov, 49, felt a sharp pain in his leg while standing on Waterloo Bridge. He saw a man pick up an umbrella, apologise and get into a taxi. Markov died four days later. A tiny metal pellet was discovered embedded in his thigh. It had possibly contained ricin. The British police inquiry remains open and the pellet is kept in the secure conditions of the Crime Museum.

◄ Photograph of pellet from Georgi Markov's leg, 1978.

PORTLAND SPY RING 1961

In 1961 the Portland Spy Ring was broken when five people were convicted of plotting to pass secrets to the Russians about Britain's nuclear-powered submarine programme. On 7 January, Harry Houghton, Ethel Gee and Gordon Lonsdale were arrested at Waterloo. On the same day Peter Kroger and his wife Helen were arrested at their Ruislip bungalow. Houghton and Gee were sentenced to fifteen years in prison, Lonsdale to twenty-five years and the Krogers to twenty years. In 1964 Lonsdale was exchanged for British spy Greville Wynne and in 1969 the Krogers were exchanged for Gerald Brooke.

MICRODOTS — MOUNTED as found in the handbag of Mrs Kroger

three flowers

TALCUM POWDER

Richard Hudnut
LONDON · NEW YORK · PARIS

▲ **Microdots** containing a letter in Russian found in Helen Kroger's handbag. Microdots are minute film negatives which can contain vast amounts of information and are easy to hide. Peter Kroger's antiquarian book business allowed him to send them abroad hidden in books.

◄ **Tin** found in the Krogers' bathroom. Its cap unscrews to reveal hollow compartments either side of a central reservoir of talcum powder. One contained a microdot reader. The bathroom could be used as a darkroom.

▲ This **microdot reader** was found in the talcum powder tin. It was used to view information on microdots.

▲ **Batteries** in the Krogers' torch were found to be hollow. One battery contained $6,000 in $20 notes.

▶ The man known as **Gordon Lonsdale** was identified as Soviet agent Konon Molody. Molody had taken the identity of Gordon Lonsdale, a Canadian who died in about 1943. It is believed that his papers were stolen by Soviet agents for use by their spies.

▼ This **cigarette lighter** was found in Lonsdale's flat. Its concealed metal container held negatives, prints and signal pads for codifying messages.

▶ This **flask** contains two hidden cavities. Iron oxide powder, used for reading Morse code recorded on tape, was found in one. After their arrest the Krogers were identified as Morris and Lona Cohen, who were wanted for spying in America a decade earlier.

BURGLARY & ROBBERY

▼ **False footprint makers**, mid-twentieth century. A burglar stamped these into the ground as he was approaching and leaving premises to suggest to police that a person with smaller feet was responsible for his crimes. However, he left his own footprints alongside the false ones and was caught.

In nineteenth-century London late summer was known as the 'burglary season' because many houses were left unoccupied as families went on extended holidays. The Crime Museum's main purpose at this time was to inform officers about burglars' techniques. Its first catalogue entry was a set of jemmies (crowbars) for housebreaking.

Objects in the museum's collections reveal the Metropolitan Police's role in investigating burglaries and robberies, including the Great Train Robbery in 1963. In 2000 the force foiled an attempted diamond robbery at the Millennium Dome in Greenwich. If the robbers had succeeded it would have been the world's biggest robbery.

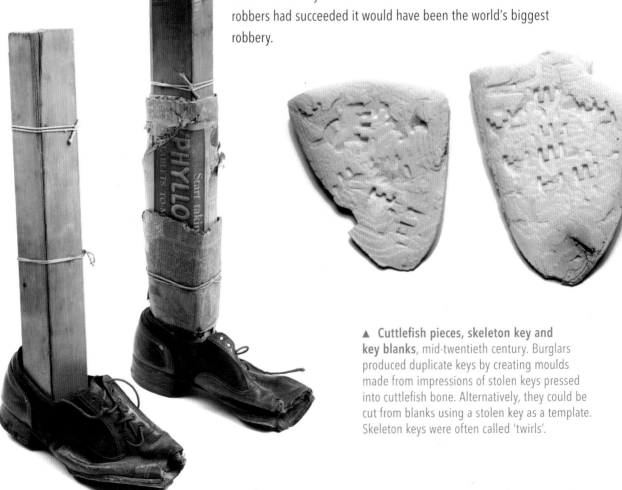

▲ **Cuttlefish pieces, skeleton key and key blanks**, mid-twentieth century. Burglars produced duplicate keys by creating moulds made from impressions of stolen keys pressed into cuttlefish bone. Alternatively, they could be cut from blanks using a stolen key as a template. Skeleton keys were often called 'twirls'.

▲ **ATM theft equipment**, 2011. This ATM card-copying equipment was seized by police near Kensington High Street. It uses a mobile phone camera hidden behind a plastic panel above the keypad to record PIN numbers being entered. Although the panel is designed to blend in with the ATM machine, a tiny viewing hole for the camera is visible.

◄ **Welder's face mask**, late twentieth century. As safes became stronger during the nineteenth and twentieth centuries, thieves began to use new technology such as blow torches and explosives to break into them. Thefts of explosives could often be connected to safe break-ins.

THE GREAT TRAIN ROBBERY 1963

The Glasgow-to-London mail train was raided on 8 August 1963 near Cheddington in Buckinghamshire. The fifteen-man gang boarded the train, which they knew contained used banknotes being sent for destruction at the Royal Mint; the train driver, Jack Mills, resisted them and was beaten over the head. When the gang's driver failed to move the train, Mills was forced to drive the uncoupled packages coach to Bridego Bridge, where the gang unloaded £2.5 million. They then travelled to Leatherslade Farm, 28 miles away.

Detective Chief Superintendent Malcom Fewtrell, head of Buckinghamshire CID, requested support from Scotland Yard and a CID team was dispatched, under Detective Chief Superintendent Gerald McArthur. The team included Leonard 'Nipper' Read, who would later investigate the Krays. Detective Chief Superintendent Tommy Butler, head of the Flying Squad, led the London investigation with a six-man team, which included Detective Sergeant Jack Slipper. Slipper would later try to arrest Ronnie Biggs in Brazil.

The gang's hideout was quickly discovered. They had left in a hurry when they found out the police were on their trail, leaving abandoned vehicles from the robbery and fingerprints. With this evidence and their knowledge of London's gangsters, the Met officers quickly caught most of the gang. Three of the leaders initially evaded arrest: Bruce Reynolds and Buster Edwards escaped to Mexico, while Jimmy White went on the run in Britain. The trial of the others was held in Aylesbury Assizes in 1964, with most members of the gang being sentenced to thirty years' imprisonment each. Some sentences were reduced on appeal. Charlie Wilson and Ronnie Biggs escaped from prison. By 1970, however, all the men had been caught, with the exception of Biggs, who eventually escaped to Brazil. Although Biggs became the most well-known of the gang, he actually had been quite a minor player.

▲ **Monopoly money** found at the farmhouse.

▲ Official **paper money wrapper**, found abandoned at the farmhouse.

▲ **Items left at Leatherslade Farm**. The robbers left the farm in a hurry, leaving their fingerprints on many objects. The small keyhole-shaped stickers indicate the presence of fingerprints. These were produced as evidence.

METROPOLITAN POLICE

On the 8th August, 1963, the Glasgow to Euston mail train was robbed of about two and a half million pounds.

Substantial rewards will be paid to persons giving such information as will lead to the apprehension and conviction of the persons responsible.

The assistance of the public is sought to trace the whereabouts of the after described persons:

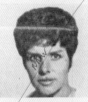

RONALD EDWARDS alias RONALD CHRISTOPHER EDWARDS, also known as "BUSTER," aged 32, florist club owner, 5ft. 6in., stocky build, complexion fresh, hair dark brown, eyes brown, London accent, scar left of nose and right forearm.

JUNE ROSE EDWARDS, nee ROTHERY, aged 30, 5ft. 3in., hair black. May be accompanied by daughter NICOLETTE, aged about 3 years.

BARBARA MARIA DALY, nee ALLAN, aged 22, 5ft. 1in., hair brown. May be pregnant and accompanied by daughter LORRAINE PATRICIA, aged 1 year.

JOHN THOMAS DALY, aged 31, born at New Ross, Eire, antique dealer, 5ft. 11in., complexion fresh, hair dark brown (wavy), eyes blue, scar right of forehead.

BRUCE RICHARD REYNOLDS, alias RAYMOND ETTRIDGE and GEORGE RACHEL, aged 31, born London, motor and antique dealer, 6ft. 1in., complexion fresh, hair light brown, eyes grey (may be wearing horn-rimmed or rimless spectacles), slight cleft in chin, scar left eyelid, cheek and right forearm.

FRANCIS REYNOLDS, aged about 24, 5ft. 4in., slim build, hair brown.

ROY JOHN JAMES, aged 27, born London, silversmith, 5ft. 4in., medium to slim build, complexion fresh, hair light brown, eyes hazel. Is a racing car driver.

JAMES EDWARD WHITE, alias JAMES BRYAN and JAMES EDWARD WHITEFOOT uses many aliases, aged 43, born Paddington, London, cafe proprietor, 5ft. 10in., slim build, complexion sallow, hair and eyes brown, may wear moustache, Royal Artillery crest tattooed right forearm.

SHEREE WHITE, aged 30 to 35, 5ft. 6in., complexion light coffee-coloured, hair dark brown. May have 6 months old baby and be accompanied by white miniature poodle dog called "GIGI".

Persons having information are asked to telephone WHItehall 1212 or the ne

Printed by the Receiver for the Metropolitan Police District, New Scotland Yard, S.W.1

▲ Train driver **Jack Mills**, who never fully recovered from his injuries and died prematurely.

▲ **Wanted posters** were distributed widely. The photographs on the poster above were marked 'NNW' (Now Not Wanted) as the gang was found.

BUCKINGHAMSHIRE CONSTABULARY

£10,000 REWARD

ROBBERY

About 3 a.m. 8th August, 1963 from the Glasgow—Euston mail train

REGISTERED PACKETS

The above reward will be paid by the Postmaster General to the first person giving such information as will lead to the apprehension and conviction of the persons responsible for this robbery.

Information to be given to the Chief Constable, Buckinghamshire Constabulary, Aylesbury (Tel.: AYLESBURY 5010), or at any Police Station.

Printed by the Receiver for the Metropolitan Police District, New Scotland Yard, S.W.1

▲ **Ronnie Biggs** escaped from Wandsworth Prison in 1965, sparking a huge manhunt. Hand-tinted photographs were issued, to show what he might look like in disguise.

▶ **Ronald 'Buster' Edwards** wanted poster.

▼ **Bruce Reynolds** fingerprint record sheet. Reynolds returned to Britain in 1968 and was arrested later that year.

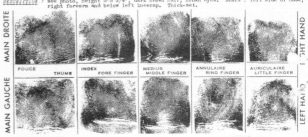

EDWARDS

Ronald.

born on 27th January 1931 in London (Great Britain)
married to ROTHERY June Rose born on 31st August 1932
OCCUPATION : florist, club proprietor
NATIONALITY : British
IDENTITY HAS BEEN CHECKED AND IS CORRECT
ALIASES : "BUSTER".- EDWARDS Ronald Christopher
DESCRIPTION : see photo, height 5'5 3/4", dark brown hair, brown eyes. Scars : left side of nose, right forearm and below left kneecap. Thick-set.

MAIN DROITE					
POUCE	THUMB	INDEX FORE FINGER	MEDIUS MIDDLE FINGER	ANNULAIRE RING FINGER	AURICULAIRE LITTLE FINGER

MAIN GAUCHE

FINGERPRINTED AND PHOTOGRAPHED IN LONDON (great Britain) on 12/5/1961

PREVIOUS CONVICTIONS :

Has previous convictions in Great Britain for attempted larceny, assault on police, etc.

MISCELLANEOUS INFORMATION :

Holder of passport n° 800944 issued in London (Great Britain) on 3/8/1963. Wanted by the British authorities in connection with the robbery of a mail train in Cheddington, Buckinghamshire (Great Britain), when approximately £2,250,000 sterling was stolen. Accomplices in this offence : DALY John Thomas, born on 6/6/1931 in New Ross, subject of international notice n° 554/63 A 4785 of September 1963; REYNOLDS Bruce Richard, born on 7/9/1931 in London, subject of international notice n° 550/63 A 4782 of September 1963; WHITE James Edward, born on 21/2/1920 in London, subject of international notice n° 551/63 A 4783 of September 1963; JAMES Roy John, born on 30/8/1935 in London, subject of international notice n° 552/63 A 4784 of September 1963.----- EDWARDS may be accompanied by his wife (holder of passport n° 800945, issued in London on 3/8/1963) and his daughter NICOLETTE, aged 2 years and 9 months.

His arrest is requested by the British authorities. A warrant will be issued immediately when the place of arrest is known. EXTRADITION WILL BE REQUESTED.

REASON FOR THIS CIRCULATION :

Done at the request of the British authorities in order to discover his whereabouts. If found, please detain, seize all property and money in his possession, and inform immediately the British Representative, International Criminal Police Organisation, National Office, Criminal Investigation Department, New Scotland Yard, LONDON SW 1 (INTERPOL LONDRES SW 1), and the I.C.P.O. INTERPOL, General Secretariat, 37 bis rue Paul Valéry, PARIS (INTERPOL PARIS).

I.C.P.O. PARIS
September 1963

File N° : 555/63
Control N° : A. 4786

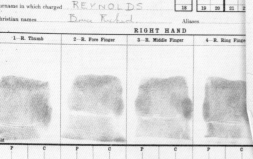

C-3 13	C.R.O. Number				POLICE		MALE 0				
		1 — 6	7 8					9	10	11	
							18	19	20	21	

Surname in which charged REYNOLDS
Christian names Bruce Richard   Aliases

RIGHT HAND

1—R. Thumb	2—R. Fore Finger	3—R. Middle Finger	4—R. Ring Finger

Fold

	P	C	P	C	P	C	P	C
28	29	30	31	32	33	34	35	36	37	38	39	40	41	42	43	44	45	46	47

Impressions to be so taken that the flexure of the last joint shall be immediately above the line marked "Fold". If the impression of any digit be defective a second print may be taken in the vacant space above it.

When a finger is missing or so injured that the impression cannot be obtained, or is deformed and yields a bad print, the fact should be noted in the appropriate space provided.

The "rolled" and "plain" impressions are to be obtained first, then prisoner should sign his name, and lastly a rolled impression of the right fore finger is to be taken on the back of the form. If that finger is missing or injured, the impression of another finger should be taken and the form amended accordingly.

LEFT HAND

6—L. Thumb	7—L. Fore Finger	8—L. Middle Finger	9—L. Ring Finger	10—L. Little Finger

THE MILLENNIUM DOME ROBBERY 2000

On the morning of Tuesday, 7 November 2000 four men crashed a JCB digger into the Millennium Dome. They were attempting to steal twelve diamonds estimated to be worth £350 million. After throwing smoke bombs and spraying ammonia gas, they broke through the display case holding the diamonds with a nail gun and sledgehammers. Flying Squad and Firearms Officers, some disguised as cleaners, jumped out, grabbing guns from bin liners. Accomplices outside were arrested. Others were arrested the next day. Kent Constabulary and the Metropolitan Police had spent months planning Operation Magician to foil the raid. In February 2002, four men were found guilty of conspiracy to rob and given long prison sentences.

▼ **Model of Millennium Dome,** made to a scale of 1:2000. It was donated to the Crime Museum by De Beers.

▲ **Replica Millennium Star diamond.** The previous day the real diamonds had been replaced with replicas made by De Beers. The original diamond, considered to be the finest jewel in the world, was valued at £200 million. It had played a key role in the Dome's opening celebration on New Year's Eve 2000.

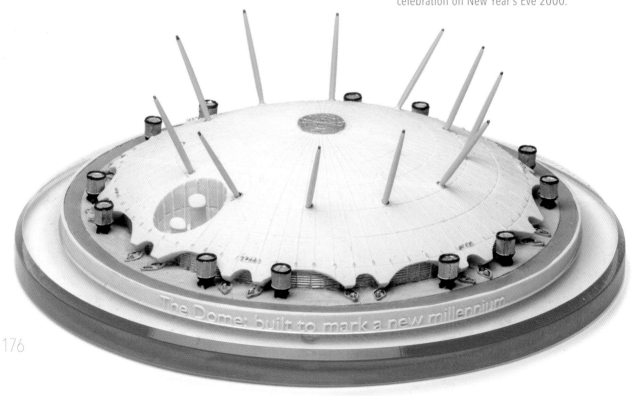

COUNTERFEITING & FORGERY

Items relating to counterfeiting and forgery have been central to the Crime Museum's collections from its earliest years. In 1899 they filled two or three display cases and were frequently mentioned in journalists' reports.

By the middle of the twentieth century some counterfeit coins and forged banknotes were so well produced that even bank officials were deceived. Many of the objects in these cases highlight the great skill and attention required to detect counterfeits and forgeries.

▲ **Plaster mould** inside wood and metal screw press.

▲ **Counterfeit jewellery and 'gems'**, c.1960s–1980s.

COINING EQUIPMENT

In 1902 a journalist listed the tools required for producing counter-feit coins. These were 'a melting pot, iron ladle, files, lampblack and grease, an electric battery, brushes and moulds and a good coin, usually old and worn down in places, from which to obtain the impression'. He went on to describe the process of making counter-feit coins: 'an impression is taken and ... molten metal is poured in through the sides of the mould and the mould is clamped together until the coin is set. The coiner then files away the tail or "get".' Next the coiner milled the coin's edges with a file and knife and 'silvered' it in a battery. The finished coin was burnished with a 'scratch' brush and polished with lampblack and grease, which was then washed off. Coiners often worked in spaces where they would have warning of unwanted guests – for example, up creaky stairs.

The whole process remained largely unchanged for much of the twentieth century.

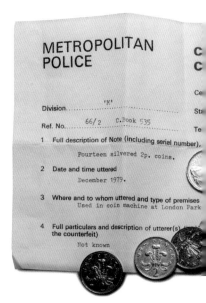

▲ **Counterfeit coins.**

◀ **Mould** for 50p piece.

▼ **Metal sheet** from which blank 50p coins have been cut out.

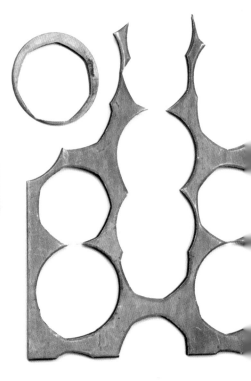

▶ **Type used for counterfeiting**. After the Second World War opportunities for forgery increased as documents such as cheques, postal orders, savings bank books, insurance stamps and season tickets became more widely used.

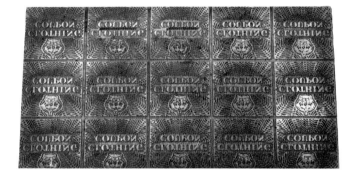

▼ **Printing press, printing plate and counterfeit clothing coupons**. In June 1941, two years after food rationing started, clothes rationing began. During this time ration coupons and books were a valuable commodity and ripe for forgery.

FORGED BANKNOTES

In the nineteenth century, the most popular denominations were £5 and £10. Counterfeit notes would be crumpled and soiled to make them look old and used.

The invention of photography allowed work that used to take days to be done in a few hours. Forgers were often experts in photography, lithography and platemaking, and many notes almost defied detection. Sometimes several printing processes were used to create a single note, including lithography, recess printing from a copper plate, and letterpress printing for the numbering.

▼ **Banknotes** forged by Frederick Beckert. In the 1930s forged notes handed into banks were passed to Scotland Yard for comparison with other forged notes. They were then cancelled by writing or stamping the word 'forgery' across them and finally surrendered to the Bank of England.

FREDERICK BECKERT

In 1938 the Bank of England discovered high-quality forged bank-notes from France. Detective Inspector George Hatherill travelled to Paris, where a man had been arrested for trying to change English banknotes. Painstaking detective work led Hatherill back to London where he identified the man as a German national called Frederick Beckert. In June 1938 Beckert, 40, was convicted of forging banknotes to the value of £5,000 and sentenced to four years' imprisonment. After his release he was interned as an alien and then deported.

▲ Beckert's **alien registration card**.

▶ **Printing plate** made by Beckert.

▼ **Sheet** showing one stage in the process Beckert used to forge notes.

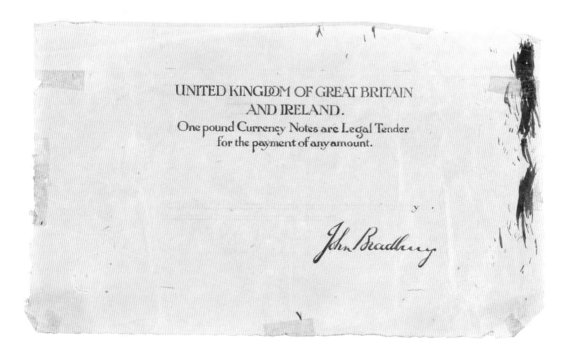

POLICE PROCEDURES

COLLECTION OF EVIDENCE

There have been huge developments in the methods used to collect and process evidence over the last hundred years. During the twentieth century the importance of the forensic pathologist to a criminal investigation grew. This was partly due to an increased realisation of the strengths of scientific evidence, but it was also because of the emergence of a number of famous pathologists.

Perhaps most famous was Home Office pathologist Sir Bernard Spilsbury, who worked on cases such as those involving Hawley Crippen, Patrick Mahon and Gordon Cummins. Others included Professor Keith Simpson, who worked on a number of high-profile cases, such as those of Neville Heath and John Haigh, and Professor James Cameron, chair of Forensic Medicine at St Bartholomew's Hospital from 1973 to 1992.

▲ **Pathology case** belonging to Professor James Cameron.

▶ **Murder bag**, late 1940s to 1950s. In 1924 Sir Bernard Spilsbury noted that detectives working at the Emily Kaye murder scene were not wearing gloves, despite the fact that they were sorting through burnt human remains. He instigated what became known as the murder bag – a bag that detectives could take with them to an investigation which contained everything they needed for collecting evidence, such as bags, gloves, tape measures, containers and so on. This example dates from the late 1940s to 1950s but has had equipment added to it as required.

▼ **Plastic evidence tube**, 2000s. Today evidence is collected in a range of specially designed containers. The length of this plastic tube can be varied to allow it to contain different-sized objects.

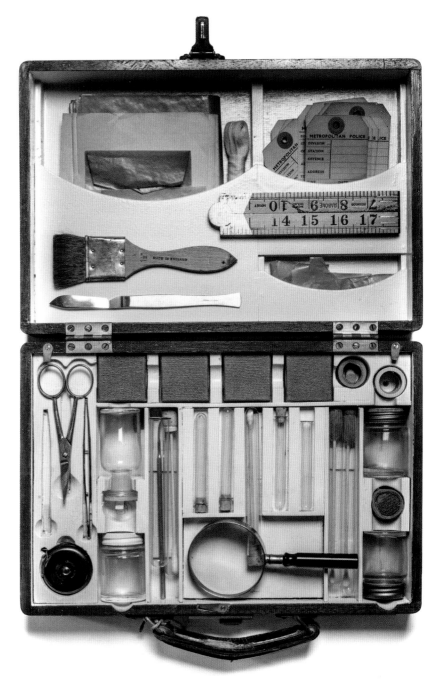

DETECTION

When the murderer Daniel Good escaped in 1842 and went on the run for ten days, the embarrassment that was caused led the Metropolitan Police to found the first detective branch in England. In 1878 it was reorganised into the Criminal Investigation Department (CID). Over the years many of the detectives have become as famous as the criminals they investigated.

Up until the late twentieth century, information about criminals and police procedures was communicated by printed booklets, wanted posters and word of mouth. The *Police Gazette*, produced weekly since the 1770s and daily from 1914, was supplemented by larger illustrated circulars. In addition, each police officer was issued with instruction books to which they could refer. Many were mini-folders so that additional information sheets could be added as they were issued.

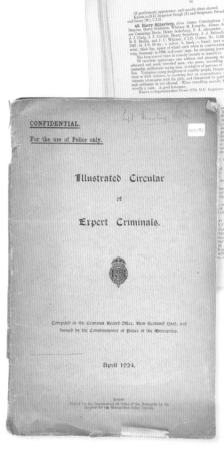

▲ **Illustrated Circular of Expert Criminals**, 1924, and **Special Illustrated Circular of English, Colonial and Foreign Expert Criminals**, 1911, showing known suspects accompanied by descriptions and notes.

◄ **Police War Duties Manual** 1965, issued to officers during the Cold War, advising them on what actions to take in the case of a nuclear war.

◄ By the 1960s and 1970s **small pocket manuals** were produced; which included photographs of both criminals and common types of weapon.

EARPRINTS

While fingerprinting has been a proven method of identification since the beginning of the twentieth century, the use of earprints has yet to become as widespread. Fingerprints have distinctive ridges and patterns which are unique to each of us. Earprint identification relies on the fact that everyone's ears have different shapes or different anatomical features.

This panel of glass is a very early example of an earprint being used as evidence in a court case. It came from a ground-floor window at a builder's firm in Kentish Town in 1968. The premises had been burgled and the police recovered the earprint and items left behind by the burglar. Some months later they arrested a man for a similar crime. His ear, when compared, was very similar to the print. However, the police laboratory examined a hundred other ears and found that three were also similar. The jury found the man not guilty of the earprint robbery but guilty of the second crime.

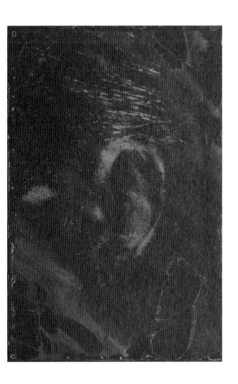

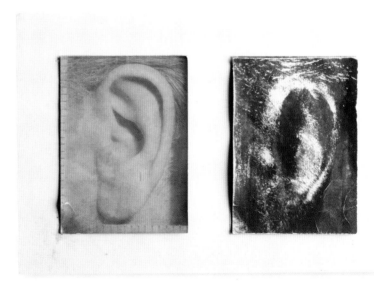

IDENTIKIT AND PHOTOFIT

Facial composite systems are a means of building up an image of what a suspect may have looked like. Initially this was done by a witness describing to an artist what the suspect looked like, but by the 1950s in America this had evolved into a sophisticated construction system known as Identikit. By 1970 this had been replaced by Photofit. Today computer- based systems, such as E-FIT (Electronic Facial Identification Technique), are more widely used.

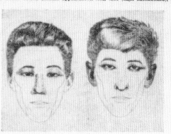

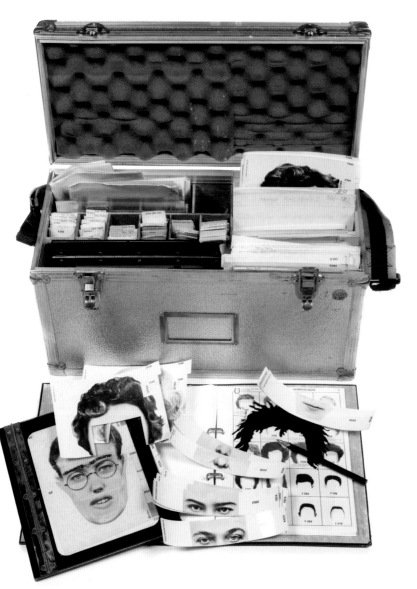

▲ **Wanted poster** for Edwin Bush using an Identikit image. Identikit was first used in London in 1961 by Detective Sergeant Raymond Dagg. He produced this image of Edwin Bush from two different witness descriptions. Bush was wanted for the murder of Elsie Batton. The image led to his arrest and ultimately to his conviction and execution.

◄ **Aluminium Photofit case** holding black-and-white photographic reproductions of facial features. The witness could build up the face of the suspect using these sets.

▲ This variant of **Photofit** used colour photographic images.

COURTROOM SKETCHES

Court cases are occasionally televised today, but in the vast majority of cases in Britain the privacy of the judicial procedure is preserved and the only images from the courtroom are those prepared by the court artist. William Hartley's sketches from the late nineteenth to early twentieth centuries allow a glimpse of what court procedures were like.

Before the invention of photography, sketching was allowed in the courtroom. By the 1920s there was increasing unease about photography in court and in 1925, partly in response to the Patrick Mahon trial, photography and sketching were completely banned from the courtroom and its precincts. Even today court sketch artists can only make notes in the courtroom and have to do their drawings outside. In 2013 artist Priscilla Coleman was the first artist to make drawings in a court since 1925 when she was allowed to sketch during an appeal hearing in the Supreme Court.

▼ **Courtroom scenes** sketched by William Hartley during the trial of Robert Wood for the Camden Town Murder, 1907. Wood, an artist, was acquitted after a brilliant defence by Sir Edward Marshall Hall.

CONCLUSION

CONCLUSION

So where now for the Metropolitan Police's Crime Museum? The New Scotland Yard building has been sold and the Metropolitan Police are moving to new headquarters. Assurances, however, have been given that the Crime Museum will move with it and will continue in existence. And this is a good thing. We need a Crime Museum. We may not be comfortable with that idea, but we do. Crime, in all its guises, is a constant and we need to have people – curators and archivists – who keep and record this material. Why? Because crime is as much a part of human life as anything else is.

By producing this book and exhibition we have brought forward the stories of so many forgotten people who should not have been forgotten. When discussing crimes we so often use the shorthand of the murderer's name; the murderer becomes the defining character of the crime. The victims, however, remain nameless and voiceless. Nowhere is this seen more than in the Jack the Ripper case, where the murderer is unknown and yet how many people can name the murdered, even though their names are known? It would be naive to expect there to be a huge change, but it would be good if we could at least think more often of the victims when we look at these crimes.

In working on this project we read about hundreds of offenders, victims, detectives – all those involved in these cases. In the beginning, the 'famous' cases stood out, but now it is the 'un-famous' cases that remain. Emily Barrow (page 41) walked to work one morning in 1902, having left her violent common-law husband a few days before. She probably didn't see him following her until it was too late and he stabbed her. She died on the street in Shadwell, another victim of 'domestic' abuse. Sadly, the truth is that her story could have happened yesterday, today or tomorrow, anywhere

▲ **Maud Marsh**, last victim of the Borough Poisoner (see page 46)

around the world. And this is why we need a Crime Museum. So that we remember.

But there are also other reasons why the Crime Museum's collections should continue to exist and to be added to. Crime in London, as elsewhere is changing and evolving. Cyber-crime is today's buzz term, but soon this will evolve into something else. Alongside new crimes, older ones continue but evolve. The Krays and the Richardsons in the 1960s have been replaced by different types of gang crime – the same sort of crime, but evolved to a different level in a different London. In such a diverse city, new crimes emerge as new communities settle and become part of it. Female genital mutilation (FGM) and so-called 'honour' crimes are a feature of crime today in London. And the Crime Museum is already collecting items that reflect these newer crimes. The current curator works closely with detectives, to follow up on cases as they develop, exploring what will be reflective of crime in London today.

There is also a role for the Crime Museum as the keeper of developments in detection methods and forensics. Many of the cases detailed in this book are there because of these developments: the Stratton Brothers as the first murderers convicted on fingerprint evidence in 1905; the changes in the law regarding the taking of images in court after Patrick Mahon's conviction in 1924; the role of the media and a psychiatrist in helping the police bring about an end to the Spaghetti House siege in 1975. There is a need for the evidence of these new developments to be retained and displayed. Today we take fingerprint evidence for granted, but, along with the development of identification through DNA, it must rank as one of the major developments in crime-fighting. Criminal cases from the Crime Museum's collections involving the use of DNA were too recent for inclusion in the exhibition or this book, but if we were to repeat the exhibition in fifty years' time, they would undoubtedly feature.

Finally, there is the role of the museum itself. A museum displays objects or items from its collections to tell a story. Objects are strong transmitters and the visitors' closeness to a real object is what makes museums special. This is all the more so with the Crime Museum. The objects in its collections are incredibly powerful. They bring a sense of immediacy and relevance that cannot be gained through images or films. They are also, often, very ordinary, even mundane objects – a kitchen knife, a stocking, a scarf. And these, because of their ordinariness, are often all the more terrifying – much more so than guns or crossbows, which for most of us it is hard to imagine being in our daily lives. Most of the objects in this book, and in the Crime Museum, have undergone a journey within which their meaning has changed. They have moved from domestic or personal items to become part of the evidence for a criminal investigation. When they come into the Crime Museum they change again into something that has been part of a criminal case but is also removed from it: they have become museum objects, but also they stand as mute witnesses, if that is not too hackneyed a phrase. The power of the object to relate a story, and to bring us into that story, is very real in a collection such as this.

The police will continue to use this collection to teach their new recruits: about the history of the Metropolitan Police, about the sense of continuity of the force within the lives of Londoners, about the types of crime that they will confront, and the challenges they will face. So the Crime Museum will continue to fulfil this function. For us, as visitors to the exhibition and in this book, we catch a glimpse of what it contains – of lives stopped mid-flow, of hopes unfulfilled, of dreams unrealised. So, on many levels, there is a very powerful argument for retaining and maintaining a Crime Museum for London.

12/15